NEW YEAR

ITS HISTORY,
CUSTOMS AND
SUPERSTITIONS

Theodor Gaster

New Year

ITS HISTORY, CUSTOMS
AND SUPERSTITIONS

Abelard-Schuman, New York

To

OLGA AND HANS

for many New Years

We may see Time rather as a sower than as a reaper, a youth with a spade and a basket of seed rather than an ancient with a scythe; and if he keeps his sand-glass, it is of the nature of a sand-glass that when it runs down it can be turned over and started again.

VISCOUNT SAMUEL

Contents

List of Illustrations

Foreword

NEW YEAR is at once the oldest and the most universal of all festivals. There is scarcely a people, ancient or modern, savage or civilized, which has not observed it or does not observe it in one form or another. Yet no other festival has been celebrated on so many different dates or in so many seemingly different ways.

This book attempts to describe the customs, traditions, beliefs and superstitions which have gathered around New Year from the earliest times to the present day. The more one examines them, however, the clearer does it become that these observances which seem at first sight so different and diverse are really no more than variations upon the same theme; and that though the accompanying emotions may have changed and though he may be completely unconscious of this fact, the behavior of the modern sophisticate on New Year's Eve or New Year's morn stems ultimately from the same roots as does that of his more primitive brethren.

To preserve this unity and to present the picture in proper perspective, it has been found best to adopt, in the following pages, a *topical* rather than a *regional* treatment. Each chapter is therefore devoted to a different aspect of the festival rather than to a separate description of, say, the Christian, Mohammedan, Chinese or other New Year. The only exceptions are the accounts, in Chapter 15, of the Babylonian New Year and, in Chapter 16, of the Jewish festival of Rosh Hashanah. The former has been treated separately because it is the earliest New Year celebration of which we have detailed record, and the latter because it presents several unique features not to be found elsewhere.

The story has been told in plain, straightforward style. The writer has found, for his own part, that honest, unvarnished accounts of what other peoples do and think are always more reliable and more interesting than the "quaint" and precious embellishments which so often characterize books on folklore. In the belief that other readers will share this preference, he has carefully eschewed any gilding of the lily.

A special point has been made, however, of introducing, at appropriate places, ample specimens of popular New Year songs and jingles; and in this connection particular attention may be invited to the verse renderings of the Babylonian hymns which have been made by the writer especially for the present volume.

New Year is not only the oldest and the most universal of festivals; it is also, in a sense, the parent of them all. More than a mere accident of the calendar, it is a triumphant reassertion, from year to year, that Life is in the end victorious and that Death is swallowed up forever.

NEW YEAR

ITS HISTORY,
CUSTOMS AND
SUPERSTITIONS

❧ 1 ❧

Days of Our Years

So teach us to number our days
That we may get us an heart of wisdom.
Psalms 90:12

THE STORY OF NEW YEAR'S DAY BEGINS, ODDLY ENOUGH,
at a time when there was as yet no such thing as a year.
For primitive men measure their existence not in rounded
twelve-month cycles but in vague and discontinuous
times and seasons—periods when the moon waxes and
wanes, when the crops must be sown or reaped, when
the animals rut or yean, when "the flowers appear on
the earth, and the voice of the turtle is heard in the land."
To the Tupis of Brazil, for instance, the largest unit of
time is the period when the wild geese honk, and to the
Algonquins of Virginia it is that which elapses between
one blossoming of the cashew tree and the next.

· 1 ·

Often, of course, a number of these shorter spans are combined to make up a longer spell—a season of heat or cold, of rainfall or drought, of intensive activity in the fields or of forced idleness at home. Even this, however, does not produce a continuous year, for those seasons are not necessarily added together, nor is it always realized that they come round in cycles. The Eskimos of Greenland, for example, recognize only the winter, and the Seminole Indians of Florida only the summer; while in parts of Borneo, those who live in the plains take account only of the eight or nine moons of the wet season, and those on the plateaus only of the six moons from sowing to reaping. All the remaining time is regarded by these peoples as "dead" and left entirely uncomputed. Similarly, in some of the South Pacific islands, there is a season of the southwestern monsoon and another of the northeastern; yet, though they in fact succeed each other, they are always treated as individual units and never as parts of a larger whole. In Dahomey (French West Africa) the nearest equivalent to our rounded, comprehensive year is a term which means literally "time-of-reaping-maize-and-eating-it-plus-time-of-planting-it-again-and-reaping-it-again"!

Moreover, even when the primitive *does* realize that times and seasons revolve, he reckons the cycles separately, and therefore still possesses no standard calendar year. The Melanesians, for example, recognize as many such separate cycles as there are different crops, just as the Connecticut farmer speaks of a "corn year," a "wheat year," and so forth, and just as the Jewish Talmud asserts that there is one year for crops, a second for animals, a third for trees, and a fourth for measuring the reigns of kings!

What now survives only among rude and primitive peoples was once the common practice of mankind. The best evidence of this is the fact that our own word *year* really means *spring-time*, showing clearly that our ancestors measured time by seasons. Similarly, in the ancient Sanskrit language of India, the word for *year* originally denoted *autumn*, and in that of South Arabia it referred primarily to *the season of plucking dates.* The Slavs and Norsemen reckoned time by winters; and the Greeks spoke habitually of a "one-*winter* goat" when they meant that the animal was one year old. The Teutons, for their part, had to fall back on the cumbrous expression "summer-plus-winter" in order to convey the notion of a continuous year; while the Incas of Peru (or, at least, the poorer folk among them) appear to have regarded the harvests as the standard major units of time. Nor, indeed, should it be overlooked that even today popular idiom still speaks of "a girl of fifteen *summers*," unconsciously preserving a trace of the earlier usage.

It is one thing, however, to recognize spans and seasons; quite another to determine when they begin. The first swallow does not always arrive, nor the first snow fall, at precisely the same time; and neither can be told in advance. Primitive Man gets over this difficulty by a simple but ingenious device: he gears the beginnings of seasons and cycles to fixed *astronomical* phenomena—that is, to the position and movement of the sun, moon and stars.

Spring, for example, is usually reckoned from the rising of the Pleiades, that cluster of seven stars which is one of the most conspicuous features of the heavens. Among several primitive peoples, that event serves as the signal for sowing crops, and hence as the beginning of the entire agricultural cycle. Alternatively, the season is reckoned from the moment when the sun rises at the same point on the horizon as does the star Altair; and among the ancient Egyptians, the year commenced (in July) with the heliacal rising of Sirius, the brightest star.

Again, the crucial date may be the vernal or autumnal equinox, or the new moon nearest to it. The Babylonians, for example, reckoned their year (according to two alternative systems) from the new moon in mid-March or that in mid-September, and the Jews followed suit; and before the Julian reform of the calendar, the Romans likewise adopted the former of these two dates. Indeed, until comparatively recent times, the vernal equinox was generally regarded in European countries as New Year's Day, and in England the civil, as distinct from the historical, year still begins on March 25!*

Sometimes, on the other hand, it is the winter solstice that is regarded as the logical beginning of the year, because it is then that the sun begins to increase in strength. This system is especially common among peoples, like the Koryaks of Siberia, the East Greenlanders, and the Eskimos of Hudson Bay, who happen to live in arctic climes. But it also explains why our own New Year falls on January 1: this date (which came to us *via*

* France changed to January 1 only in 1564; Holland, in 1575; Scotland, in 1660; Protestant Germany, in 1700; Russia, in 1706; England, in 1752; and Sweden in 1753.

the Julian calendar) was chosen originally because of its proximity to the winter solstice.

As civilization progresses, the need for a single stabilized year, in place of the diverse seasons and cycles, becomes more and more imperative. What may have been adequate for the primitive no longer remains so for his descendants. Peoples living in different areas and under different climatic conditions come, through marriage, slavery, trade and travel, to establish relations with one another; local communities merge or become absorbed (either voluntarily or through conquest) into larger states; common religions are adopted and common festivals observed. When these things happen, sheer necessity dictates that a single standard calendar be established. Accordingly, the old system of reckoning time by the phases of nature gradually falls into the discard, because the phases are not uniform in every place. Instead, a purely artificial system is adopted: the seasons are reckoned, formally and officially, from a fixed astronomical date, regardless of whether or not it actually coincides always and everywhere with the true beginning of a natural phase. In modern terms, summer comes in on June 21 though not one swallow may yet have arrived, and furs may be worn after Thanksgiving, no matter what the actual temperature may be.

Moreover, at this stage of his development, Man has usually come to realize that Time is an infinite sequence and that its seasons revolve. He therefore no longer measures it in short disconnected spans but rather in rounded continuous cycles, from one occurrence of the date in question until it comes round again. In other words, times and seasons yield place to *years*.

Nevertheless, old customs die hard, and popular usage clings tenaciously to more primitive modes. The beginnings of the seasons retain their hold as the crucial moments in the life of the world. Though not officially recognized as such, each remains a virtual New Year, and continues to be observed with all of the ancient rites and ceremonies which originally ushered in the new lease on life. Such festivals, therefore, will have perforce to be included in our story.

ॱ2ॱ

Grave and Gay

To modern man, new year's day is primarily an occasion for fun and frivolity. Its standard celebration is a party, and the scene of its observance is as often as not a night-club or bar. To our remote ancestors, however, and to our more primitive brethren of the present day, it is an extremely serious business; for on it depend, in a very real sense, the issues of Life and Death.

Primitive Man thinks of life not as a progression from the cradle to the grave but as a series of leases; and New Year's Day (or the beginning of a season) is to him the time when the lease falls in and has to be renewed. The renewal, however, does not come automatically by law of Nature or grace of God, for of such things the primitive has no conception. Rather it has to be fought for and won by the concerted efforts of men. If the sun is to go on

· 7 ·

shining, the rain to fall in due season, man and beast to multiply, and crops to increase, human effort must be enlisted. To organize and co-ordinate this effort, and to ensure that the maximum energies be employed, a formal program of rites and ceremonies is established under communal and religious sanction; and it is this program, shorn of its original function and garbled almost beyond recognition, that really underlies the traditional pattern of our own New Year celebrations.

The program falls into four parts. First come rites of *Mortification.* When the old year is drawing to a close and the lease on life is running out, Man is, so to speak, at the end of his rope—faint, languid and exhausted. Rites of mortification express this state. They take the form of fasts, lents and other austerities. Normal business is suspended; no marriages are solemnized; and no litigation is conducted. The king, as the vessel and steward of the community's life, is formally deposed—sometimes even slain—and a temporary substitute holds office until he is reinstated or a successor appointed. Everything is topsy-turvy; and days of mortification themselves are often regarded as outside the calendar.

Next come rites of *Purgation,* the object of which is to rid the community of all evil (physical and "moral" alike) which might threaten or impair its chances of continued life. Demons and malicious spirits are formally exorcized, and the spirits of Death and Blight are expelled. Men and beasts, and even houses and barns, undergo a thorough cleansing and aspersing; temples are scoured, and their worn-out vessels and furnishings replaced. Often, a human or animal scapegoat is dis-

patched out of the community in order to carry away
evil and contagion.

The ceremonies of purgation pave the way for those
of *Invigoration*—that is, for the positive procedures which
ensure the renewal of life. These rites take various forms.
One of the most common is the staging of a mock combat
between Life and Death, Summer and Winter, Rain and
Drought, Old Year and New—the antagonists being represented either by individuals or by teams. On the issue of
the combat depends, of course, the continuance of life
and fertility.

Another form is indulgence in sexual license. This is
believed not only to increase the human population but
also, by what is called "sympathetic magic," to influence
the growth of animals and crops. Men and women are
permitted—nay, encouraged—to abandon themselves to
what Boswell so delightfully styles "the Cyprian passion";
and their king is required to undergo a ceremony of
symbolic "marriage" with a chosen temple votaress. The
cruder excesses of the modern "carnival spirit" are—believe it or not—very largely a survival of these more func-
tional procedures!

Furthermore, fires are lit and water libations poured
in order, as it is thought, to rekindle the sun and precipi-
tate the rain for the coming year.

Finally come rites of *Jubilation*. The new life being
now assured, the mood of anxiety changes to one of
relief—expressed in cordial reunions and in general feasting and merriment. The feasting, however, is inspired, at
the same time, by something more than mere conviviality.
By breaking bread together, people cement their ties of

kinship. The banquets therefore serve also as a means of confirming the solidarity of the group.

In the forward march of civilization, the pristine urgency of these ceremonies has long since disappeared. Knowledge of natural laws or belief in the providence of God has largely removed the necessity of relying on human efforts to secure the order of the universe. New Year's Day and the beginnings of the seasons are therefore regarded at the present time as mere accidents of the calendar or, at best, as occasions for prayer and thanksgiving. Nevertheless, the ceremonies by which they are observed are still, in large part, relics of things which were once done in far more solemn mood and for a far more serious purpose. The ringing of bells, the tooting of horns, the firing of rockets, the wearing of masks, the exchange of hats and the telling of fortunes, innocent as they may seem, really go back to the gray dawn of civilization, to a time when Man was more afraid of Nature than of his fellow man.

3

Year's End

THE ROMAN GOD JANUS, WHO PRESIDED OVER THE MONTH of January, derived his name from the word *janua*, meaning "door." Since a door leads both in and out, Janus was always portrayed with two faces: one looking backwards, and the other forwards. Janus is a fitting symbol of New Year ceremonies; for these ceremonies are designed just as much to get rid of the past as to welcome the future. They belong, in fact, just as much to the old as to the new; and it is in the last days of the old year that they usually begin.

It is a common practice in many parts of the world to mark the end of the year by a brief period of suspended animation, everyone behaving as if he or she were half dead. Fasting and other forms of austerity become the order of the day, and all normal activity is held in abeyance.

In Cambodia, for example, the new year is introduced (in March) by a three-day suspension of normal life, while during the first seven days no living thing may be killed, no business transacted and no litigation conducted. Similarly, among the Creeks, Cherokees and Choctaws of North America, the New Year festival (in August) is called "the Fast," and no food is eaten for two nights and one day until the new crops have been tasted.

Among the Mao Naga of Manipur, a period of abstinence and taboo is observed for four days at the reaping of the harvest—the virtual beginning of the year; and this practice obtains also in South Massam, New Guinea, and Peru, and among the Natchez Indians.

In Hawaii, the New Year festival (in November) is inaugurated by a four-day "lent," when it is forbidden to go bathing or fishing or even to blow on conchs. The high priest is blindfolded and remains in seclusion. On the fifth day, there is a brief respite; the priest's bandages are removed, and canoes are permitted to put out to sea. On the morrow, however, the "lent" is resumed for a further twenty days.

The Muhso of Burma close their villages to strangers during a five-day period beginning at the Chinese New Year. If any outsider enters, he is kept prisoner, and dispatched, on the sixth day, without his clothes, the presence of a foreign element being regarded as an impediment to the community's chances of renewing its life.

The Ossetes of the Caucasus keep a one-month term of abstinence around harvest time in order to induce the demon Tutyr (really a distortion of St. Theodore of Tyre!) to restrain his wolves and spare the sheep.

More familiar examples of the practice are the Ramadan of the Mohammedans and the Christian Lent. Although, in the manner of religious festivals everywhere, each has been re-interpreted in terms of a particular tradition, it is generally accepted by scholars that they go back ultimately to more primitive seasons of mortification at the end of the year. During Ramadan, the faithful Moslem must abstain from eating, drinking, taking snuff, and every worldly pleasure, until sundown. Indeed, he is not even permitted intentionally to swallow his saliva!

Another example is afforded by the well-known Twelve Days of the European popular calendar. Usually, these are reckoned from Christmas to Epiphany, but that is only because a more ancient institution has been deftly re-interpreted by the Church. Survivals of the earlier pre-Christian usage are still, in fact, to be found. Thus, in the Celtic areas of Scotland and France, the Twelve Days are often counted not from Christmas but from New Year; while in Silesia, they immediately *precede* Christmas, preserving the last traces of an abstinential period before the winter solstice. These days are everywhere characterized by a deliberate inversion of the normal order of things and often by a suspension of work. In the Frisian Islands, for example, all carts and wheelbarrows used to be laid up, on the ground that it was forbidden to turn wheels while the wheel of time itself was at a standstill.

The custom is attested also in ancient civilizations. Among the Babylonians, for instance, the first ten (or even sixteen) days of the year were observed as a kind of lent. No litigation could be conducted; physicians were not allowed (at least, on some of these days) to cure the sick; fishing was forbidden; and the powers of the king were temporarily curtailed. Similarly, in Greece, the festival of Thesmophoria, which served as a kind of feast of renewal at the beginning of autumn, was characterized by fasting; and in Cyprus it was preceded by a nine-day lent. Among the Hebrews, the Festival of Ingathering was prefaced by a solemn Day of Purgation which included a fast and a stoppage of work; and to this day, Jews observe special restrictions during the ten days between New Year and the Day of Atonement. In Phrygia, the death and resurrection of Attis, the god of fertility, was celebrated annually in March, and the celebration was introduced by a period of fasting and austerity, designed to represent the temporary eclipse of all life upon earth.

Not infrequently, the period of suspended activity is regarded as "outside time," and is not reckoned among the days of the year. The Aztecs, for example, used to append to the normal year a special period of five days known as "unfit for work," during which all religious ceremonies and civic business came alike to a standstill. Similarly, the Mayas of Yucatan recognized five supplementary days called "days without name," when all heavy work, and even personal ablutions, must be avoided.

In order to symbolize that, throughout this period, the life of the community is virtually at an end, the king, who is normally regarded as the vessel and steward of it, is temporarily deposed, another person reigning in his stead.

This custom is of hoary antiquity. In ancient Babylon, the king was formally humiliated at the New Year festival. The high priest stripped him of his robe and other insignia, made him kneel, and then solemnly boxed his ears and tweaked his nose. Only towards the end of the festival was the monarch reinstated. Among the Persians, one of the royal domestics was installed as temporary king during the festival of Sacaea, in July; and in Rome, February 24 was known by the mysterious name of "Flight of the King," which is thought to point to an ancient custom of expelling the king during the days immediately preceding the New Year of March 1.

In modern Cambodia, the king abdicates for three days in February, and during that time his place is taken by a substitute. Similarly, in Siam a temporary king is appointed at the end of April, or the beginning of May, while the real king remains confined to his palace. So, too, in the kingdom of Jambi, in Sumatra, each reign is inaugurated by the preliminary installation of a temporary king; while in Samarcand such a monarch rules for a day at the beginning of the year, and in upper Egypt he holds sway for three days during the time when the Nile is at its highest. Temporary kings are likewise appointed, at major seasonal festivals, among the Kwottos of Northern Nigeria, the Bakitara of the Uganda Protectorate and the Bastar of the Central Provinces of India.

Sometimes, however, the last days of the year are given over not to austerity but, on the contrary, to abandon, the idea being that during this period normal life is not so much in abeyance as topsy-turvy. Public offices cease to function; slaves are permitted to lord it

Twelfth Night revels

over their masters; and a spirit of license and revelry prevails.

In Scotland, where this mode of observance is especially common, the Twelve Days are indeed known as "the Daft Days," and are characterized by boisterous merriment and by every inversion of the normal order of things; and the German *Fastnacht* and the English

Fasten's E'en as popular names for Shrove Tuesday derive from a word which really means "to play the fool," and thus bespeak the same usage.

In this gayer mode of celebration, the temporary king takes the form of a Lord of Misrule whose function is to preside over the ceremonies from Christmas Day until Twelfth Night. Even those grave seats of learning, the universities of Oxford and Cambridge, used annually to elect one of their Masters of Arts to this office; and in the Inns of Court in London, appointment to it was regarded as a prized social distinction. We are informed, in fact, that in 1635 the person chosen was so flattered by the honor that he spent no less than two thousand pounds on providing entertainment for the public and, as a reward for his bounty, was subsequently knighted by Charles I.

In country districts, the lord of the manor would confer the title on one of the gentleman of the county. The following, for example, is an extract from such "articles" of conferment drawn up by the Right Worshipful Richard Evelyn, Esq., father of the author of the *Diary*, appointing and defining the functions of a Christmas Lord of Misrule over his estate at Wotton, Surrey:

> *Imprimis,* I give free leave to Owen Flood, my trumpeter, gentleman, to be Lord of Misrule of all good orders during the Twelve Days. And also, I give free leave to the said Owen Flood to command all and every person or persons whatsoever, as well servants as others, to be at his command whenever he shall sound his trumpet or music, and to do him

good service, as though I were present myself, at
their perils ...

I give full power and authority to his lordship to
break up all locks, bolts, bars, doors and latches,
and to fling up all doors out of hinges, to come at
those who presume to disobey his lordship's com-
mands.
GOD SAVE THE KING.

Nor was this custom unknown even to the cloister.
Prior to the Reformation, it used to be the custom in
Scottish monasteries to elect an Abbot of Unreason to
preside over the Christmas and Twelve Day revels. Readers of Walter Scott's "Waverley" novels (are there any
left?) will recall the vivid description of one of these
mock ecclesiastics in *The Abbot.* In 1555, however, the
annual burlesque was formally proscribed by act of the
Scottish legislature.

4

Good Riddance to Bad Rubbish

WHEN THE PERIOD OF AUSTERITY OR TOPSY-TURVYDOM IS at an end, men are ready to meet the new year. There can be no new year, however, until the old is formally disposed of, no new life until death is banished, no increase or prosperity until blight and contagion have been removed. The disposal of the old year, the banishment of death, and the removal of blight and contagion therefore form a cardinal element of New Year celebrations in all parts of the world.

As a rule, the ceremony is performed in a literal manner, an effigy of the dread power being solemnly paraded through town or village and then buried, drowned, or burned. Different peoples perform it, of course, on different dates, but it is everywhere related to that season of year which is regarded as the end of one lease on life and the beginning of another. In this sense, therefore, it is essentially a New Year usage.

On the Isle of Guernsey, for example, it used to be the custom, on December 31, to parade a crude dummy through the parishes and then bury it on the seashore or at some equally unfrequented spot; this was called "burying the fag-end of the year." Similarly, at Dobschwitz, in Austria, young people used to march in procession through the village on March 1 (the old New Year's Day), carrying an effigy made of straw and dressed in old clothes. This effigy was known as "the Death," and was subsequently drowned in a neighboring stream, the ceremony being believed to protect the district from plague and sickness during the ensuing year.

In Bohemia, children used likewise to carry a straw puppet to the end of the village during the month of March, the while they sang:

> Death we carry out
> Far beyond the pale;
> Summer bring we in;
> Little green shoots, hail!

Then they burned it and returned singing:

> Death we've carried out;
> Life we've brought along.
> He's come to dwell among us,
> So greet him with a song!

In Franconia (Germany), it was customary at mid-Lent—a season which coincides, more or less, with the ancient beginning of the year—for country girls to carry through the villages a miniature coffin containing a small effigy, which they subsequently threw into a nearby stream, to the accompaniment of the doggerel chant:

> If we bore him not away,
> Death throughout the year would stay.

At Bielsk Podlaski (Poland), the image of Death, made of plaited hemp and straw, used to be carried through the town at the same time of year, and then drowned in a neighboring marsh or pond. Those who took part in the ceremony made a point of running home as fast as their legs could carry them; if anyone stumbled, it was a sure sign that he or she would die during the course of the year.

The Sorbs of Upper Lausitz had the custom of fashioning a similar puppet out of straw and rags. The woman in whose family the latest death had occurred was required to supply a shirt to clothe it, and the most recent bride had to furnish a veil as well as the necessary rags. The puppet was mounted on a long pole, and the most buxom wench of the village rushed along with it at full speed, while the rest of the company sang:

> Proud and high you twirl around,
> To fall at last upon the ground!

The dummy was then pelted with stones and eventually drowned in a stream or tossed over the boundary-line into the next village.

An analogous custom prevailed also in parts of Thuringia, where a puppet made of birchen twigs was borne around the villages on the fourth Sunday in Lent, and subsequently thrown into a pool. The accompanying jingle declared that

> Beyond the shepherd's hut we wend,
> Here at Death's own funeral.
> Evil powers are at an end;
> Summer now is with us all!

In the eastern regions of Silesia, the image was actually known as Marzana, the goddess of death in the ancient pagan religion of Poland.

Something very similar takes place, at the present day, in several parts of Morocco, where the "funeral" of "Father 'Aishor" forms a prominent feature of the great 'Ashura, or New Year, Festival. Throughout the preceding ten days, from the moment when the new moon first becomes visible, young girls scratch their faces in mourning and send up the continuous wail, "Father 'Aishor has died!" On the day of the festival itself, they take a date and, after smearing it with water, saffron and pounded roses, wrap it in calico and then solemnly inter it or throw it down a well. This represents the formal disposal of the old year.

In Spain and Italy, an even more grotesque custom prevails. At mid-Lent—that is, at the old beginning of the year—a puppet, made to represent the oldest woman in town, is paraded noisily through the streets and then sawn through the middle. The ceremony is called "Sawing the Old Woman," and is taken to symbolize the final dispatch of the dying year. At Barcelona, it was a common thing, in the early part of the nineteenth century, to see large groups of boys racing through the thoroughfares armed with saws and billets of wood. As they ran, they would sing a song declaring that they were looking for the oldest woman in the place and intended to saw her in half. In due course they would pretend to have found her, and start sawing the billets. The latter would then be consigned to the flames.

Similarly, in the highlands of Scotland, the decrepit old year is burned at the beginning of Yuletide, a straw dummy known as "the auld wife" being tossed into the fire.

Often, the dispatch and "funeral" of the Old Year is followed, in short order, by his "resurrection."

In Rumania, for example, it is customary, during the Dog Days of August, when all life seems to have gone to sleep, for parties of girls to go out of the villages carrying, under a pall, a miniature coffin in which is deposited a clay image called Kalojan (see picture, page 46), or Beautiful John. Strewn with mint, basil and other aromatic herbs, the coffin is subsequently buried at a lonely spot, and for two days the girls keep singing dirges like these:

Jan, Kalojan,
as our tears drop,
so may the rain drop,
to fill the ditches and water the grass.

Jan, Kalojan,
your mother, broken-hearted,
is seeking you thro' woodland and glade.
Jan, Kalojan,
your mother is shedding for you
searing, burning tears.

On the third day, however, the coffin is disinterred, and the "resurrected" Kalojan is led back to the villages amid great rejoicing.

The same thing takes place also in the Abruzzi, where the figurine is known as *Pietro Pico*, or Peterkin; and in Little Russia, the burial and revival of Kostrubonko, the spirit of fertility and genius of the year, was celebrated annually in spring, the ceremony coinciding (through Christian influence) with the season of Easter. Here, too, the performers were girls. One of them would lie on the ground as if dead, while the others would move slowly around her in a ring, chanting the doleful refrain:

> Dead is our Kostrubonko, dead!
> The one we loved is dead, is dead!

Suddenly, however, the "corpse" would spring up, whereupon the "mourners" would at once change their tune and break out into a joyful song of triumph and exultation:

> Our Kostrubonko comes to life!
> The one we loved now comes to life!

Ceremonies of this kind are the last lingering survivals of what was once a widespread method of "seeing out" the old year and "seeing in" the new; for the burial and resurrection of little figures representing the Spirit of the Year or the Lord of Fertility is well attested as a seasonal rite in ancient times.

We are told, for instance, that at the great Egyptian festival which ushered in the spring, it was customary to fashion images of the "dead" god Osiris out of vegetable mold and spices. These were then watered and the subsequent emergence of green shoots was taken to symbolize that the god had revived. Similarly in Syria, small images of Adonis, lord of fertility, were buried every year and then (apparently) exhumed in order to simulate the annual "death" and revival of vegetation. Plutarch informs us that in the first century of the common era, when exotic Oriental cults became fashionable in Rome, it was quite a common thing for Roman women to stage a mock funeral of Adonis around the time of the vernal equinox; and it would appear that the obsequies were followed, after a few days, by a ceremony of resurrection. "On a specified night," says another contemporary writer, "an effigy is laid supine on a bier, and rhythmic dirges are recited over it. Then, when the people have had their fill of this mock lamentation, a light is brought in, and the throats of the wailers are anointed by a priest. This done, the priest whispers softly:

> Good cheer, ye votaries! The God is saved,
> Which means we too are saved from all our ills!"

An ancient Canaanite poem recently discovered at Ras Shamra, on the north coast of Syria, and dating in its present form to the middle of the second millennium B.C., appears to be based on a ritual pantomime performed in an even earlier age, during late September or early October, when the summer drought comes to an end and the new lease on life begins with the onset of the rainy season. The theme of the poem is the conflict between Baal, god of rainfall and fertility, and Môt, god of death; and at one point in the story, Môt is represented as being formally banished to the nether world and the waste places. Evidently, then, the Canaanites knew of an annual or periodic expulsion of Death, like those which we have decribed.

Old Year and Death, however, are not the only victims of this ignominious treatment. Just as often, it is the spirit of blight and pestilence, or evil demons in general, that are formally driven out of the community at those crucial and critical seasons when the new lease on life is thought to be beginning.

Among the Wotyaks of eastern Russia, for example, young girls forgather on New Year's Eve (or on the following day), carrying special sticks with which they beat every corner of the house and yard, crying out: "We are driving Satan out of the village." Sometimes, too (as Sir James Frazer tells us), the ceremony is carried out in more drastic fashion. After offering a sacrifice to the Devil at noon, men come on horseback to the center of the village and thence proceed from house to house, scourging out the Evil One with whips, bludgeons and blazing faggots, the while they yell wildly and spit on him. Then they ride at full speed out of the village, as if chasing the Evil One before them, spit on him once more, and finally throw their bludgeons away.

In Siam, guns are fired on the last day of the year in order to frighten off the demons. The first shot is fired from the palace, and the salvo is then taken up by successive intermediate stations until it reaches the outer gate of the city. Thereupon a rope is tied around the circuit of the walls, to serve—in a literal sense—as a *cordon sanitaire* and prevent the re-entry of the spirits.

The Japanese make a practice of casting out devils at

the great feast of Setsubun, which marks the end of winter and (theoretically) of the natural year. An official exorcist runs through the streets crying, "Devils out, good fortune in!" and rattles a wand in order to scare the evil powers away. Invited into the houses, he strews dried peas and beans around in the four directions. These are subsequently swept up and preserved. They are cooked when the first clap of spring thunder is heard.

Among the Eskimos of Point Barrow, Alaska, it is customary to expel the evil spirit Tuña at the moment when the sun reappears on the horizon after its winter absence, for it is then that the new lease on life is thought to begin. Parties of young women chase the demon out of the houses by stabbing at everything with long knives, while older women, posted at the doors, brandish weapons to prevent his re-entry. Once he is supposedly ejected, he is driven towards a fire in front of the central council-house, around which the elders of the tribe stand in a semi-circle. Each recites a formal list of charges, brushes his clothes to avoid contagion, and bids the monstrous being leap into the flames. A shot is then fired, and a pot of urine tossed on the blaze. As the steam rises, a second shot rings out, and this marks the final discomfiture of Tuña—at least until the following year.

In the Indian archipelago, the riddance of evil takes on an even more bizarre form. Around the time of the vernal equinox—the real beginning of the year—it is loaded symbolically upon a raft, which is then left to drift out to sea. Similarly, in the Nicobar Islands, demons are driven onto a model ship at the beginning of the dry season, and the vessel is then cut loose from its moorings. This is called "Dispatching the Devil by Sail."

Another way of banishing evil at the beginning of the year is to load it upon a *scapegoat,* animal or human, and then kill that unfortunate being or scourge it out of the community.

The Bible tells us, for instance, that at the beginning of the ancient Hebrew year, five days before the autumnal Feast of Ingathering, there was celebrated a great Day of Atonement, and that on this occasion the high priest used to take two goats and cast lots over them, "one lot for Jehovah, and the other for Azazel."* The goat upon which fell the lot of Jehovah was promptly slain as a sin-offering; over the other the high priest laid his hands and, confessing all the iniquities and transgressions and sins of the children of Irsael, symbolically transferred them to it. The animal was then driven into the wilderness, to bear the uncomfortable burden to "a solitary land."†

In much the same vein, it was formerly a common New Year custom in parts of Breadalbane, in Scotland, to lead a dog to the door, give him a bit of bread, and then expel him, crying, "Away, dog! Whatever death of men or loss of cattle might otherwise befall this household during the course of the year, be all of it transferred to you!" At Barea, in the Hebrides, a cat or dog is driven out of doors, with a bunch of lighted straw tied to its tail.

Sometimes, however, the scapegoats are human beings. In Siam, for example, it used to be the custom, once a year, to make one of the loose women of the city

* The meaning of this name is unknown. It is presumed to denote a demon of the desert.

† Leviticus 16:5-22.

serve as a scapegoat for the entire community by parading her through the streets on a litter and then flinging her on a dunghill or hedge of thorns. The unfortunate creature was believed to attract to herself all evil and mischief which might otherwise alight upon the populace during the course of the year. Also, at Onitsha, on the Niger, all persons who have committed gross offenses during the year club together to purchase two sickly persons, who are sacrificed as human scapegoats. One of them is for the land, the other for the river; and—significantly enough—the execution has to be performed by an outsider who is not a member of the community.

Analogous rites are attested also in ancient times. The Babylonians used to parade and scourge a human scapegoat at the New Year festival; and it would appear that in parts of Greece two condemned or misshapen persons, one male and the other female, were annually scourged out of the city, and perhaps also burned or stoned, at the great Thargêlia festival in May.

Lastly, there are cases where the scapegoat is neither animal nor human, but a mere dummy. In Korea, for example, anyone who is about to enter a critical year of his life makes a straw effigy on the fourteenth day of the first month, dresses it in his own clothes and then leaves it on the roadside. Whatever happens to the cast-out image is supposed to happen to the man's former self, now gone into the past.

The same general theme of driving out evil at the beginning of the year belongs to the common European custom of expelling witches during the critical twelve days between Christmas and Epiphany or at the commencement of the summer season in May. In Bohemia, for example, it is customary, on New Year's Eve, for boys to form circles and fire three times into the air, the purpose being to shoot down the witches as they come riding on their broomsticks. In Silesia, shots are fired over fields and ploughlands on New Year's Eve in order to scare away the same sinister workers of mischief, while fruit trees are wrapped in straw to prevent harm at the hands of demons.

In the Tyrol, houses are cleansed and fumigated on the last three days of April, and bundles of resinous faggots are burned as a means of "smoking out" witches. Our own familiar "spring cleaning" is, in reality, nothing but a faint survival of these more primitive usages.

Crude and naive as the expression may be, behind these diverse and curious rites there lies the common human feeling that a new year means a new life; a consciousness, as Gilbert Murray has expressed it, "that man, though he desperately needs bread, does not live by bread alone, but longs for a new life, a new age, with young gods, not stained by the deaths and impurities of the past."

∾5∾

When the Fur Flies

IT IS NOT ALWAYS POSSIBLE TO GET RID OF THE OLD YEAR or of the forces of evil simply by expelling them. Sometimes they will offer resistance, and the issue has then to be decided by a battle royal.

In many a Rhineland village, says Grimm, it used to be the custom, at the end of spring, for two persons, one wearing ivy to represent Summer, and the other straw or moss to represent Winter, to stage a public combat, and to go on fighting until Summer eventually downed his rival. Similarly, in Styria and in the neighboring mountains of Carinthia, two bands, one with winter clothes and snowballs and the other with green summer headgear and pitchforks, used to engage in a mock battle towards the end of March or on the feast of St. Mary's Candlemas; and at Voitzenburg, in the Ukermark district, a fight between Summer and Winter was (or is) staged on Christmas Eve, the antagonists being impersonated, as a rule, by old women.

In Sweden, two companies of mounted troops, the one dressed in furs and the other in fresh leaves and flowers, used to stage a set-to on May Day; the latter, representing the forces of Summer, naturally won. Fights between Summer and Winter were likewise a regular feature of midsummer ceremonies in several of the villages of Russia; and among the Iroquois, the New Year festival, held in late January or early February, includes a mimetic combat between the Spirit of Life and Fertility (Teharonhiawagon) and that of Winter (Tawiskaron). Contests of the same type also characterize the two great tribal festivals held by the Yakut of Turkey in spring and autumn. On each occasion, Spring, called "the good spirit," comes dressed in white and riding a white horse and engages Winter, the "bad spirit," who is clothed in red and rides a roan horse. An analogous procedure marks the Basque Carnival masquerade at La Soule, in southern France, where *Les Rouges* fight *Les Noirs*.

Nor are such combats by any means confined to modern times. Herodotus, that seemingly inexhaustible mine of ancient custom, informs us that the Egyptians used likewise to stage an annual "fight with clubs," at which, so he avers, "They bash each other's heads in, and, so I think, many even die of wounds." Such a fight is, indeed, actually portrayed on a relief in the tomb of Kheryaf at Thebes. So, too, in Mexican ritual, the priest of the maize goddess, dressed grotesquely in the skin of a

The seasonal combat in ancient Greece
(From the tomb of Kheryaf, at Thebes)

newly slain animal, engaged in combat with a troop of soldiers at the annual festival of that deity.

In course of time, as civilization progresses and men lose their pristine innocence, both the urgency and the significance of these jousts tend to fade, and they come to be re-interpreted as commemorations of historic encounters. This tendency is attested in both ancient and modern times.

The Egyptians, for instance, used to stage a mock combat as part of the annual festival of the god Sokar, which was celebrated at Memphis in December, but they regarded it as the re-enactment of an earlier battle between factions in the city of Buto, the predynastic capital. The annual ritual combat among the Hittites was taken to commemorate some early border clash between themselves and their neighbors, the Maeonians. Plutarch, in his "Life of Alexander," describes an analogous mock combat between two teams identified as the followers of that monarch and his rival Darius respectively; and it is not without significance that even to this day, folk-plays introducing an "Alexander of Macedon" are still performed, during Christmas week, in parts of Scotland.

In several English villages, a mimetic battle which is fought at Hoketide (i.e., on the Tuesday following the second Sunday after Easter) is popularly interpreted as commemorating a fight between the English and the invading Danes; but at Jedburgh, on the Scottish border, where it has degenerated into a football match played annually on Fastern's E'en, it is taken as the memorial of a fierce battle between the Scots and the English at nearby Ferniehurst Castle.

Sometimes, too, the combat is given a *local* setting without being historicized. Thus, at Gambach, in Hessen (Germany), it takes the form of a battle between the inhabitants of that village and those of the neighboring hamlet of Griedel; and at Slitrig, in Scotland, the opposing teams consist of men from the western and eastern banks of the river respectively. Similarly, the annual fight at Edinburgh, on Shrove Tuesday (a crucial seasonal date), is between the "uppies" and "doonies" —that is, between men living above Mercat's Cross, towards Castlehill, and those living below it, towards Townfoot; while at Ludlow, in England, it is the men of the Corn Street Ward and those of the Broad Street Ward who annually contend in a tug-o'-war on the same date.

Finally, there are cases where the combat survives simply as a traditional institution without any rational attempt to explain it, whether by historicization or by localization. At Scone, Scotland, for example, bachelors contend at football against married men on Shrove Tuesday, but no one knows why or wherefore. Similarly, in "merrie England," it used to be the custom on May Day for one village to contend with another in dancing-matches, each side raising the cry, *Hey for our town!*

Garbled, distorted and forgotten as they may be, all

of these New Year and seasonal contests are but the lingering survivals of what was once a very real and serious battle between Life and Death.

ᴐ6ᴐ

Sticks and Stones

Dʀɪᴠɪɴɢ ᴏᴜᴛ ᴛʜᴇ ᴇᴠɪʟ ɪs ᴏɴʟʏ ᴏɴᴇ sɪᴅᴇ ᴏғ ᴛʜᴇ ɴᴇᴡ Year ceremonies. Equally important is it to drive in the good; and the curious thing is that much the same methods are used for the latter as for the former.

Just as you can beat out evil, so you can beat in good —an idea still perpetuated by unprogressive parents who speak of "beating sense" into their unruly offspring.

In sundry villages of England, especially in the counties of Devonshire and Sussex, it is customary for young boys (known as "howlers") to rise early on New Year's morn and visit the orchards. Encircling every apple tree, they proceed to beat it with rods of willow and to chant in chorus:

Stand fast, bear well, top!
Pray God send us a howling crop;
Every twig, apples big;
Every bough, apples enow;
Hats full, caps full,
Full quarter* sacks full!

The custom is prevalent also in other parts of the world. In the Tyrol, for example, all fruit trees are violently beaten with clubs or staves, and sometimes even pelted with stones, at the beginning of the Twelve Days between Christmas and Epiphany; and the same usage is reported from France, Germany and Belgium. In New Caledonia, it is a regular practice to beat plants in order to make them grow; and on the seventh day of the Feast of Booths—the ancient fruit harvest—Jews used to strike the ground with willow sticks. Indeed, the Talmud quotes one of the earlier sages as observing that "every blade of grass has its prescribed destiny, and for each there is an angel in heaven who beats it and says, Grow!"

Sometimes it is not merely the trees or plants that are struck, but human beings themselves. In rural districts of Germany, for instance, men and women often treat one another to special "smacks" with willow branches (*Ostersmacken*) at Easter or the beginning of spring; and the Jews of Tripoli strike their fellow-worshipers rather than the ground at the Feast of Booths.

The practice goes back to remote antiquity. In the Greek city of Ephesus, for example, the human scapegoats who were expelled annually at the festival of Thargêlia in order to drive *out* evil† were at the same time

* I.e., quarter of a hundredweight.
† See page 29.

• 38 •

trounced with branches of willow as a vicarious means of driving *in* fertility; and at the Roman festival of Lupercalia (on February 15), two young men of good family had to run at full speed around the boundaries of the old Palatine settlement, clad only in loincloths, and strike at everyone they met with thongs of goat's hide. This was believed especially to deliver women from barrenness.

The purpose of the ceremony was to rouse the indwelling spirits of fertility at moments when they were thought to be dormant or sluggish. The Greek poet Theocritus (third century B.C.) tells us, in fact, that it was customary in Arcadia to belabor the images of the rustic god Pan whenever food became scarce; and by the same symbolism it is considered propitious, in many parts of the world, to administer a few token slaps on the behind to a bride immediately after her wedding!

There is, however, a less drastic method of accomplishing the same end. Fertility and bliss can be *poured over* a person or thing—an idea which underlies the anointment of kings and priests and which survives also in popular idiom when we speak of the effusion of divine grace or of the pouring out of the Spirit upon all flesh.

In the western counties of England and in certain parts of Wales, trees are ceremonially aspersed on New Year's Day. Processions are formed in the early morning, and the boughs are sprinkled with cider, while the villagers chant:

O tree, O tree, O tree,
Bear fruit and flourish,

Thy owner nourish!
Give wealth and plenty!

The custom is known fancifully as "wassailing the trees."
In Hungary, water in which the festival meal has been
cooked is used instead of cider. The symbolism, however,
is in both cases the same: the liquid (like the oil of
anointment) is believed to be possessed of a special
power of "virtue" which is thus transmitted, the choice of
cider being influenced, of course, by the fact that what
is especially sought is the fertility of the apple trees.

∽7∽

A Clean Start

VIOLENCE IS NOT THE ONLY MEANS BY WHICH MANKIND can achieve bliss. Grace can be poured as well as hammered into the human soul, and the limpid waters which cleanse impurity can at the same time infuse salvation. Indeed, to primitive peoples cleanliness is next to godliness in a very special sense. For if a man is dirty, he is possessed by the Devil, and to cleanse him is not merely to promote his physical well-being but also—and more importantly—to free him from the clutches of evil powers.

Now, as we have seen, the close of the year is a time when such evil powers are especially at large, and it is also a time when the accumulated weight of their impurity lies heaviest upon men. It is essential, therefore, that the new year begin with a clean start, and to this end rites of cleansing are everywhere a prominent feature of New Year ceremonies.

The most obvious method is ablution. In Madagascar, for instance, and likewise in Burma, everyone pours water over his or her head on New Year's Day; and a like custom obtains also in Persia. In Japan, all persons who have married during the previous year are sprinkled with water on January 2; and among the Armenians, there is a general aspersion at the Feast of the Transfiguration, which takes place during the last days of the year.

In Macedonia, not only human beings but also buildings and yards are sprinkled with water freshly drawn from the well; and in Morocco, water is poured over human beings and animals, and likewise upon the walls and floors of all dwellings, at the New Year ('Ashura) festival on the tenth day of Muharram. Likewise, it is customary among the Hindus to wash down the exterior of the house at the Duwalee festival, which marks the end of the mercantile year.

The custom is very ancient. In Egypt, sacred buildings were ritually aspersed during the annual celebration of the death and resurrection of Osiris—a virtual New Year festival; while in Mesopotamia, the sacred emblems of the temple were cleansed and scoured during the month of the New Year, and on the fifth day of the festival, an elaborate rite of purgation was performed in the sanctuary. A similar practice prevailed also among the Hebrews: on the Day of Atonement (really a phase of the New Year celebrations), sanctuary and people were sprinkled with water by the high priest.

Sometimes, however, the cleansing is accomplished by more drastic means. In the Mayan ceremony of *oc-na*, for example, it is customary, every January, to shatter all the clay idols and censers used in the temple during the previous year. New ones are then substituted, and the entire building is painted and refurbished. An ancient Hittite document, dating (approximately) from the thirteenth century B.C., prescribes much the same sort of procedure as part of the annual Puruli festival—a kind of New Year celebrated in late spring or early summer: the sacred fleeces used in worship had to be burned and replaced. Similarly, too, it was the practice at the Old Roman New Year, on March 1, to change the laurels which hung in the house of the *rex sacrorum* and in the Chapel of the Wards.

Nor is the custom altogether obsolete among so-called civilized peoples at the present day. As mentioned earlier, our own "spring cleaning" is simply a relic of the purification which used to take place before the beginning of the year, in March; and the fanciful may see in the old-time New York custom of moving to new apartments annually on October 1 a survival of the same primitive instinct to do away with the old and start afresh when the holiday season is over and men return, assumedly with new vigor, to the round of their normal activities.

> Ring out, wild bells, to the wide sky,
> The flying cloud, the frosty light:
> The year is dying in the night;
> Ring out, wild bells, and let him die.

Ring out the old, ring in the new,
Ring, happy bells, across the snow:
The year is going, let him go;
Ring out the false, ring in the true.

Tennyson

⟨8⟩

Infernal Noise

"It's DIN, DIN, DIN," SAID RUDYARD KIPLING, AND IN A SENSE other than he intended this is certainly true of New Year's Eve. All over the world, New Year comes in with a bang—or at least with a loud noise: a ringing of bells, a clashing of gongs, a blowing of whistles, a tooting of horns, a cracking of whips, and sometimes even a firing of guns or rockets. In so-called civilized societies, no one gives a second thought to this hullabaloo; it is simply an explosion of high spirits or, at best, a conventional way of saying goodbye to the old and of welcoming in the new. The fact is, however, that what is now a matter of high spirits was once a matter of very low ones, and what is today devilish and infernal in one sense was originally so in quite another. For the original purpose of the din and racket was simply to scare away those low and evil spirits which were believed to be roaming the earth at this most crucial and critical of seasons. Like small children and publicity men of the present day, our remote ancestors were firmly convinced that, if only you made enough noise, anything unpleasant or inconvenient could be easily driven away.

If the sexton in his belfry and the reveler in his nightclub are, by and large, totally unconscious of these deeper implications, there are nevertheless less sequestered parts of the globe where the old belief still survives in all its original force and where the seemingly ubiquitous goddess Hoopla has not yet invaded the ancient shrines. In Calabria (Italy), for example, it is still customary to ring bells throughout the month of March—the ancient beginning of the year—for the express purpose of driving out witches; and in the Tyrol, bells are rung and whips cracked on May Day for exactly the same reason. Similarly, at Brunnen, on Lake Lucerne, and likewise at Labrugière, in the south of France, the jangling of bells and the clattering of kettles is a recognized method of scaring away evil spirits on Twelfth Night. At Rottenburg, in Swabia, bells are rung on Midsummer Eve in order to forefend against demons; and in many rural areas of France, witches are expelled in this manner on St. Agatha's Day (February 6). In Japan, the advent of New Year is heralded by troupes of dancers who go from house to house and, on being admitted, proceed to make a furious noise by rattling bamboo sticks. This is regarded as an effective method of clearing out malicious spirits. An analogous custom prevails in parts of Scotland, where, on New Year's Eve, parties of boys parade through the villages, encircling every house three times and setting

Ancient calendar from Gezer,
Palestine, dividing the year
into agricultural seasons
(Tenth century, B.C.)

Kalojan

Seasonal combat in Holland, 1559 (From the painting by Jan Breughel)

up a deafening din for the purpose of expelling demons and witches. In the neighborhood of Zurich (Switzerland), and in the Falkenau district of Germany, it is (or was) the common practice for boys and girls to pace the streets on New Year's morn beating drums and kettles and blowing whistles as a means of frightening away hurtful spirits. In southern China, the demons of cholera are driven off at midsummer (one of the "natural" New Year's Days) by a ceremonial clanging of bells and gongs and a popping of crackers; and in ancient India similar measures were taken against the devils at the winter solstice. At Lippe, in Germany, May Day is "cracked in" with whips, and a similar usage is current in Cornwall (England) on March 1—the beginning of the old Celtic year. In both cases, the noise is thought to repel the demons.

To the same class of ideas belongs also the familiar Jewish custom of blowing the ram's horn (*shofar*) at New Year. Originally, this was done at the beginning of every month and at all the major seasonal festivals, and its purpose was to daunt the evil spirits which were thought to be especially rampant in the dark of the moon and at other crucial calendar dates. In precisely the same way, the Celtic May Day festival (*Laa Boaldyn*), which was celebrated until recently on the Isle of Man, was characterized by a violent blowing of horns designed to scare away the fairies and elves.

Nor, indeed, are these boisterous ceremonies by any means confined to New Year or similar seasonal festivals. Noise is regarded as effective *at all times* against the powers of darkness. Many primitive peoples ring bells or strike gongs at eclipses, thinking thereby to drive away the demonic monsters who are believed to be swallowing up the sun or the moon; in medieval Europe church bells were pealed during thunderstorms as a means of repelling malevolent spirits, and in the rural areas of Germany, farmers used to give special doles of corn to the local sextons to make sure that they would "ring away" the lightning from the crops. Indeed, ancient church bells often bear such inscriptions as *Lightning and thunder I break asunder*; and in Christian countries it was commonly believed that the Devil was deprived of his powers, and elves and witches put to flight, at the sound of the consecrated bell.

On the same principle, too, bells are rung and gongs clashed at moments of personal and individual crisis; for likewise on such occasions the demons are thought to be at large. Thus, among the Mandaeans of Iraq, when a woman is in labor, those who attend her ring handbells in order to scare away the forces of evil from attacking mother and child; and the same practice is reported also among the Bogos of Abyssinia. In Togoland (West Africa) the native priests ring bells as a means of exorcizing diseases from the sick.

Of the same order are the wedding bell and passing bell of modern usage. The former was designed originally to ward off demons from the bridal couple; the latter was tolled not for the dead but for the dying, its purpose being to frighten away the powers of darkness before they could make their final assault. Indeed, in the Eifel district of Prussia, it is still the custom to ring bells beside a deathbed; and this practice is attested also in eighteenth-century Scotland.

The power of noise as an averter of demons also underlies the universal practice of attaching tinkling instruments to the garments of priests and even, occasionally, of laymen. The Hebrew high priest, for example, wore little golden bells on the hem of his robe; and the Scripture indicates very clearly that their purpose was to protect him, during the performance of his duties, from the lethal assaults of evil spirits: "The sound shall be heard when he goeth in unto the holy place before the Lord, and when he cometh out, *that he die not.*"* At the present day bells are worn as a protective measure by the medicine-men of the Amur River area; they are likewise standard equipment for the shamans of the Gilyaks on the island of Sakhalin; and anyone who has traveled in the Near East will be familiar with the small amuletic bells worn by Arab men and women and even hung upon their beasts of burden.

Loud, discordant and cacophonous as it is, the din and uproar of New Year is thus but the faint echo of a distant thunder. Moreover, though sharply differentiated today, the chimes of the New Year bells and the racket of the New Year revels are ultimately one and the same thing. For both are devices on the part of men to beat the Devil at his own game, to frighten him with the very weapon which he himself employs, and to drown his accustomed pandemonium in one of their own making.

* Exodus 28:35.

~9~

All Our Yesterdays

ON NEW YEAR'S DAY, PAST, PRESENT AND FUTURE "BLEND
and blur." New Year affects the dead as well as the
living. For what is renewed on that occasion is not merely
the life of the present generation but the entire continuity of a people or, indeed, of the world—past, present
and future. It is, so to speak, not only the Americans of
today who enter upon a new term of existence, but America itself; and the spirits of departed ancestors therefore
take part in the proceedings. The basic idea is, in fact,
very much the same as that which inspires every college
president worth his salt to declare in his annual commencement address that "our founders are here with us
in spirit."

Moreover, New Year's Day (or, for that matter, any
major seasonal festival) is a time when the whole clan

gets together and re-cements its ties of kinship; and in the minds and hearts of the participants the link that binds them together is their common descent. Accordingly, if father and mother, grandparents and great-grandparents can no longer be present in the flesh, they at least preside in spirit over the family board.

The most familiar example of this belief is, of course, our own Halloween, which, despite its present Christian setting, really harks back to an ancient Celtic New Year festival at the beginning of winter. The institution itself, however, is of far higher antiquity. Some three thousand and more years ago, for example, the Babylonians believed that the dead revisited the earth during the first month of the year, and at the New Year festival portions of food were set out for them. In the ancient Egyptian city of Siut, it was customary to light lamps for the dead on New Year's Eve and New Year's Day, so that they might more easily find their way back to their kinsmen. In Greece, the great festival of Anthesteria, which fell in March (the first month of the year), was believed to be attended by the spirits of the deceased, and the celebration ended with the recital of a solemn formula ordering them back to their subterranean abode. The Romans prefaced the opening of the year, at the same season, by a prolonged adoration of the dead, culminating in the nine-day festival of Parentalia, or Departed Ancestors. Purple flowers were strewn over their graves, and offerings to them were placed under the thresholds, against the moment when they would re-enter their former homes.

Among the ancient Persians, the dead were held to return at the annual Feast of Tirajan. Whether the He-

brews knew of such a belief is doubtful, but it is significant that to this day Jews make a practice of visiting
the graves of parents during the month preceding New
Year; and popular tradition asserts that at the Feast of
Ingathering (which was originally the beginning of the
year), the patriarchs of Israel visit their descendants and
sit with them in the festal tabernacles (*sukkahs*) as hon-
ored guests. Similarly, too, the Mandaeans of Iraq hold
a festival of the dead at the beginning of the year, in
late September or early October.

Nor is it only in our own Halloween that this ancient
belief survives at the present day. Among the Siamese,
for instance, the dead are thought to rejoin their families
at the New Year feast in April; and the Tuaregs of the
Sudan begin the year with a ceremonial visit to the graves
of the departed. The Hopi Indians hold a major nine-day
festival at the summer solstice and believe that on the
fourth day the spirits of the dead return to the villages
and take part in the proceedings. The Zuñis of western
New Mexico, who begin the year at the same season, mark
the date by a pilgrimage to the sacred lake of the dead;
and in Bali, the first five weeks of the Buddhist year
are kept as a festival, and ancestral spirits are believed to
return.

Among the Hucul of the Ukraine, dead ancestors are
thought to return at Easter and Christmas—both of them
critical "new year" seasons. Honey is provided for them,
and the congregation kneels and prays: "O God, let all
the dead and all the lost come back and drink with us."

In Finland, the equivalent of Halloween, at the beginning of the year, is the Feast of Kauri, when the ghosts
of ancestors are invited into the house, and a sheep is

slaughtered for their regalement. Similarly, the Lithu-
anians entertain the spirits of the dead at the time of
New Year. When the family sits down to dinner, scraps
of food, called "death-gifts," are tossed under the table
for them. At the end of the repast, they are formally
exorcized in these words reminiscent of the formulas used
in ancient Greece and Rome:

> Spirits of the dead, away!
> Bless the living ones that stay!
> Grant this household peace alway!
>
> Go, for Fate now sounds the call;
> Go, but let no ill befall
> Window, stoop or barn or stall!

The belief that the dead are present with the living
on New Year's Day, or whenever the lease on life is renewed, is more than an old wives' tale. Crude as its
forms of expression may be, it is an instinctive testimony
to the fact that what is past is *not* merely prologue but
part of the living texture of the present, that nothing
is irretrievably lost, that corruption puts on incorruption,
and that yesterday never dies.

New Year, however, looks forward as well as backward.
If the dead past merges at that moment with the living
present, so too does the unborn future. And this likewise
finds expression in the ceremonies of the occasion; for
among many primitive peoples it is customary formally
to initiate new members into the tribal communion at the
New Year or major seasonal festival. Thus, among the
tribes of Viti Levu, the largest of the Fijian Islands, ini-

tiation into the *nanga*, or secret society, takes place at the New Year feast in late October or early November. Similarly, the natives of Swaziland initiate and tattoo children at the harvest festival of *incwala*, which is virtually their New Year; and in ancient Phrygia, novitiates were admitted to the communion of the god Attis at the great festival held at the time of the vernal equinox—the beginning of the year.

What was implied by these ceremonies was, of course, not only that the whole continuity of life, and not just that of the present generation, was entering a new term, but also that there could be no New Year without new blood.

～10～

Presages and Omens

NEW YEAR'S DAY IS AN AUSPICIOUS OCCASION IN MORE senses than one. Whatever happens on that day, it is held, is a portent of what may be expected during the course of the year. Popular tradition therefore lays down special provisions for doing the right things and avoiding the wrong ones.

Even though the day be observed officially as a holiday and marked by a general abstention from work, at least a few minutes of it should be devoted to one's normal occupation. Otherwise, that occupation will cease altogether, and one will lose one's livelihood, during the ensuing months. Ancient Roman farmers, for instance, used to guard against blight and ruin during the coming year by engaging, in purely token fashion, in every conceivable kind of agricultural labor on January 1, no matter whether much of it was quite inappropriate to that season. In the same spirit, too, housewives in medieval Germany were wont to ensure the fortunes of their homes during the following twelve months by sewing a few token stitches on New Year's Day—a piece of rank, "heathenish" superstition which so outraged the susceptibilities of the Church that it was roundly denounced as inspired by the Devil!

In modern times, the custom sometimes assumes diverting forms. At Brandenburg, for example, no sooner has the clock struck midnight on New Year's Eve than the city is transformed, if only for a few moments, into a veritable hive of industry, for everyone at once hustles and bustles to perform some semblance of his daily work; persons attending Watch Night services line their pockets with grains of corn which they proceed to "grind" with their fingers during the sermon.

Another "must" is the wearing of new or clean clothes. In modern sophisticated societies, this is simply a matter of fashion and convention, and "gay togs" or "Sunday best" serve no other purpose than to enhance the festivity of the occasion. Among primitive peoples, however, it is a matter of *ritual* and possesses a far deeper significance. The ancient Babylonians, for instance, insisted that not only the king but even the images of the gods be appareled in clean raiment for the New Year ceremonies; and in several Greek cults, it was customary for young girls to weave a new costume for the goddess and to present it to her at the seasonal festivals. The Romans made a point of wearing white on January 1; and at the present day, when the Creeks and Comanches assemble for their annual *Busk* festival—their nearest equivalent to New Year—everyone is required to don new clothes. A similar usage prevails also at New Year among the Hindus, the Tongans and several other peoples.

The reason for this custom or rule is that in primitive thought "clothes makyth man" in a very special sense: they are regarded as a symbol of individuality, part and parcel of a person's essential being. It is, in fact, on this account that kings have to don distinctive robes at their coronations, and that both bridal couples and the novices of religious orders are alike attired in special garb. In all such cases, what is indicated is that a new character or identity is being assumed. Accordingly, at New Year, when (theoretically) the community is reborn, or enters a new lease on life, every member of it must symbolize the fact by a change of raiment.

There is also, however, a secondary reason for this practice: the change of garments provides a convenient disguise against the assaults of those demons and evil spirits who, as we have seen, are believed to be especially rampant at this season. It is this, too, which really underlies the common custom of wearing masks or dominoes on New Year's Eve, and of removing them only after midnight has struck. Here again, what is now "harmless" in one sense was originally so in quite another: the assumption was that if only you could elude recognition, you could automatically foil the demons.

Just as important as the things which one *must* do on New Year's Day are the things which one must *not*.

One must not carry over anything of the old into the new; for all "unfinished business" will remain so throughout the year. Accounts must be settled and debts paid, if possible, before the new year begins. In Japan, this is taken so seriously that debts are customarily remitted or forgiven on New Year's Eve, everybody thus being given the chance to start afresh with a clean slate. Similarly, it is a common practice among unmarried domestic servants in Scotland to make a point of completing all tasks and assignments before the church bells ring on December 31; otherwise, so they think, their matrimonial hopes will likewise remain unfulfilled!

No borrowed article should remain in the house over New Year's Day; for this would presage dependence on others during the whole of the succeeding twelve months. Conversely, no member of the household should depart from it, nor should anything that normally forms part of it—even ashes, garbage or dirty water—be removed from it on that day; for otherwise there will be a loss in the family or in its worldly goods. At Edinburgh, this is carried to such an extreme that the more superstitious folk will not even sweep their floors on New Year's Day; and the general principle finds quaint expression in a traditional rhyme still current in Lincolnshire, England:

> Take out and then take in,
> Bad luck will begin;
> Take in and then take out,
> Good luck comes about.

Special care must be taken that no light or candle be extinguished or taken out of the house; for, according to age-old tradition, the household lamp or hearthfire is the symbol of its fortune and continuance. The Bible, in describing the doom which awaits the wicked, says more than once that their "light will be put out";* and it will be recalled that after King David's narrow escape from a Philistine giant, his followers tried to dissuade him from further adventures in the field "lest thou quench the light of Israel."† In an old Babylonian litany, a suppliant prays to his god that "the hearth which is dark and smoldering may glow again, the torch which is quenched may blaze anew"; and among the Arabs, the ruin of a man's household is often described as the extinction of his lamp. Who will not at once recall Othello's famous words "Put out the light, and then put out the light"?

Neither pockets nor cupboards should be empty on New Year's Day; else they will remain so throughout the year. Glassware should on no account be broken, since that is a presage of damage or death. All litigation should be avoided, for New Year is a time of communal regeneration, and "a house divided against itself shall not stand." Finally, no corpse may remain in the house; otherwise, there will be a further death in the family during the coming months.

Even the most trivial event of New Year's Day may contain a portent of what is to come. Divination, or the reading of omens, is therefore everywhere a prominent feature of the occasion. In German popular tradition, for example, New Year's Day is regarded as one of the *Lostage,* or "oracle days," others being Christmas, Twelfth Night, and Midsummer Day. A favorite method of "scrying" on that day is to pour molten lead or other metal into a bowl of water and then deduce omens from the shapes which it assumes. In England, this practice

* Cf. Proverbs 13:9, 24:20, 31:18; Job 18:5-6, 21-17.
† II Samuel 21:17.

is employed especially by young girls, and the various shapes are taken to indicate the trades or occupations of their future husbands.

Another common method of learning the future is to examine the ashes which remain on the hearth after the celebration of New Year's Eve. If there appear among them the impression of a human foot, with the toes pointing towards the door, this is a sign that some member of the family is destined to leave it. If, however, the toes point away from the door and into the room, an addition to the household may be expected. In this respect, it is a widespread Scottish belief that, if the hearth-fire is still burning at daybreak, prosperity will last throughout the year, whereas, if it has died down, prospects are bleak. If a live coal rolls away from it, a death or departure is imminent.

Fortunes may also be read in more curious ways. In some parts of the world, it is customary to run to the window as soon as one wakes on New Year's morn. If the first animal you see has its head turned towards you, you will enjoy a good year; if its tail, you are doomed to misfortune. Alternatively, if the animal is standing, this means luck; if lying, adversity. Lazier folk may learn their lot after breakfast by the less exacting method of *Bibliomancy*. This consists in opening the family Bible at random and placing one's forefinger upon one or other of the chapters which meet one's eye. The whole chapter is then read aloud, and the assembled company proceeds to "interpret" it as a prediction, or series of predictions, for the coming year.

Or, again, one may scan the skies. For on New Year's night, the heavens declare not only the glory of God but

Wassailing the orchards

The Padstow Hobby Horse

also the fate of men. Says the old *Shepherd's Kalender* of 1709: "If New Year's Day in the morning open with dusky red clouds, it denotes strifes and debates among great ones, and many robberies to happen that year." Nor, indeed, is it only the destiny of mankind that may be divined from such celestial signs. The weather of the whole year can be foretold from that of New Year's Day—often on the assumption that it will be the direct opposite. As an old English couplet expresses it:

If the Calends of January be smiling and gay,
You'll have wintry weather till the Calends of May.

By an extension of this principle, it is believed in many parts of Europe that the twelve days from Christmas until January 6 (Twelfth Night) constitute a kind of image or miniature of the entire year. The weather on each of these days is therefore regarded as a token of what may be expected in the corresponding month.

In English and German folk belief, special significance is attached to the sex, stature, appearance, complexion and even occupation of the first person one encounters in the new year. As a rule, it is considered lucky to meet a man, and unlucky to meet a woman; and in some parts of Germany it is regarded as good enough if one's first encounter is with a child or an ox-cart! In Silesia, it is held to bode ill if one meets a beggar, gravedigger or sexton; and in some outlying villages, the same invidious status is bestowed upon the mailman. A North Country superstition in England maintains that it is lucky to meet a man with his arms loaded, but unlucky to meet one who carries nothing. And the peasants

First-footing at Edinburgh (19th century)

of Bavaria insist that one should not meet a cat or dog on New Year's Day before one has met a human being.

These beliefs extend also to what is called the *first-foot*—that is, the person who first crosses one's threshold in the new year. Here, too, a male is always regarded as more auspicious, and it is usually required that he be dark-haired or dark-complexioned. Especially propitious as a first-foot is anyone who was born feet foremost, a man on horseback or a man with a horse and cart. Ill-omened, on the other hand, are criminals, redheads, persons with deformities or squints, and—above all— women. As an old English antiquary puts it, in describing how the ceremony used to be carried out: "Females have no part in this matter, and if a damsel lovely as an angel entered *first*, her fair form was viewed with horror as an image of death."

In order to clinch one's good fortune during the coming year, it is customary to hire persons with the required specifications to serve as pre-arranged first-footers. They are usually regaled with lavish refreshment the moment they set foot in the door. Sometimes, however, they are themselves expected to provide a token of good cheer or a symbol of good augury. In Scotland, this condition is usually satisfied by a bottle of whiskey. Elsewhere, however, the convivial yields place to the solemn. In Macedonia, for example, the first visitor after New Year is required to bring a stone—symbol of strength —or a green twig—symbol of life—and place it ceremoniously upon the hearth. In some parts of the world, a member of the family goes out and comes in again, to bring the New Year greeting. As soon as he is admitted into the house, he strews grains in every direction, and then felicitates each member of the household in turn. The strewing of the grains is regarded as an auspice of fertility and increase.

∽11∾

His Majesty the Baby

NO SYMBOL OF THE INCOMING YEAR IS SO FAMILIAR AS the New Year Babe—a favorite figure at New Year's Eve revels and a constant stand-by of cartoonists and of the less original among the designers of New Year cards.

In his modern form, the New Year Babe seems to make his first appearance in a German folksong of the fourteenth century, though even before that time it was quite common in Germany to refer to the New Year metaphorically as "the newborn one."

Actually, the New Year Babe is far older than he looks. In ancient Greece, it was customary at the great festival of Dionysus to parade a babe cradled in a winnowing basket. This was taken to symbolize the annual (or periodic) rebirth of that god as the spirit of fertility. The ceremony is portrayed on a sarcophagus now

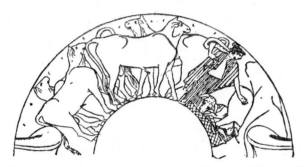

The New Year Babe in Ancient Greece: Dionysos Liknites (From a sarcophagus in the Fitzwilliam Museum, Cambridge, England)

in the Fitzwilliam Museum at Cambridge, England. Two men, one bearded, the other in the flower of youth, are shown carrying the infant in the winnowing basket; and the fact that they are depicted emerging from behind a curtain slung between trees makes it plain that what is thus represented is a scene from some open-air ritual pantomime.

A similar rite seems to have taken place at the Eleusinian Mysteries; for ancient writers record that at one stage of the proceedings the chief hierophant suddenly emerged from behind a screen and announced: "The Goddess hath borne a son." The geographer Strabo relates that the birth of Zeus was acted out annually in Crete.

Nor, indeed, is this vivid portrayal of the *renouveau* by any means confined to ancient times. Until very recently, it was a common custom in western Prussia to stage the mock birth of a child on the harvest-field; and in many parts of England and Scotland, a small sheaf of corn is tied up at the reaping and known as the "kern* baby."

So common, in fact, was the popular custom of representing the new life that the Church was eventually obliged to take it over. When the solstitial festival of the new light was transformed into Christmas—the birthday of the "Light of the World"—the New Year Babe was transformed with it into the familiar figure of the Christ Child. The little infant who had once been greeted "with trembling and perspiration" was now welcomed in quite another mood:

> Pro nobis egenum
> Et faeno cubantem
> Piis foveamus amplexibus:
> Sic nos amantem quis non redarmaret?
> Venite adoremus,
> Venite adoremus,
> Venite adoremus Dominum.†

> With marchpaynes, tartes, and custards great, they
> drink with staring eyes;
> They rowte and revell, feede and feaste, as merry
> as all pyes:

---

* *kern* (or *kirn*): corn.

† With fondest embraces
  Come, let us warm him
  Who lies for our sake in the manger forlorn.
  Who can but love him
  Who loveth us so dearly?
   O come, let us adore him;
   O come, let us adore him;
   O come, let us adore him;
    Lord Jesus, this morn!

And if they should at th' entrance of this New Year
   hap to die,
Yet would they have their bellies full, and ancient
   friends allie.

Naogeorgus

⌒12⌒

Wassail

New year's day is always a great occasion for the "inner man," and many are the special dishes and confections associated with it in different parts of the world. A feast, at which all members of a family or clan get together, is, in fact, everywhere an essential element of the festival. This emphasis on food, however, though it has often degenerated into pure conviviality, was not, in origin, a mere concession to the stomach: it possessed a far more serious significance.

In primitive custom, eating and drinking together is one of the most widely recognized methods of cementing ties of kinship or alliance, the underlying idea being that those who have partaken of food in common have thereby absorbed into themselves a common essence. Our own word *companion*, which means properly "one who breaks

The Wassailing Bowl

bread with another," is itself a relic of this ancient conception; and the practice is widely attested in ancient times in connection with the concluding of treaties and covenants. In the Bible, for instance, it is stated specifically* that when Melchizedek, king of Salem, made a treaty with the patriarch Abraham, he signalized it by proffering bread and wine; and when Abimelech, king of the Philistines, concluded an alliance with Isaac, he followed the same procedure.† Similarly, Herodotus, the "father of history" (b. 484 B.C.), informs us that among the Nasamoneans of Libya, treaties were concluded by each party's drinking out of the other's hand; and the natives of the Timorlaut Islands even go so far, at the present day, as to kill a slave and eat him jointly when they wish to establish bonds of mutual assistance!

New Year, when the family or clan embarks on a new lease on life, is the occasion *par excellence* when ties of kinship must be re-cemented; and it is this, rather than mere cordiality, that inspires the holding of the New Year feast. To be sure, the real meaning of the repast is,

* Genesis 14:18-24.
† Genesis 26:30.

as a rule, no longer remembered. There are, however, not a few instances in which its original significance survives.

In Japan, for example, all members of a family assemble at breakfast, on New Year's morn, and conclude the meal by drinking a cup of *toso* wine in honor of their departed ancestors (who are believed to revisit them for the occasion) and in order to ensure renewal of their own life and prosperity during the ensuing twelve months. The ceremony is performed in silence, and is led by the master of the house. Similarly, at Lhasa, the capital of Tibet, the dominant feature of the New Year meal is a pudding made of raisins, dried apricots and other preserves. The head of the family takes the first slice, and a portion is then doled out to each member of the company. The eating of it re-cements the ties of kinship. In the center of the pudding, a small red flag is inserted as a means of scaring off those evil spirits who might otherwise visit the family with misfortune during the coming year.

The Bible records an analogous custom among the ancient inhabitants of Palestine; for in the First Book of Samuel* we are told that Elkanah, the father of the prophet, used to make a pilgrimage once a year to the sanctuary of the Lord of Hosts at Shiloh and that on such occasions he would distribute portions of sacramental food to his two wives and to his sons and daughters.

Comparable also is the custom which used to prevail in monasteries. On the morning of New Year's Day, a bowl of wine, called the Loving Cup *(Poculum Caritatis)*, was placed at the upper end of the refectory table. The superior would then drink a toast to the assembled

* I Samuel 1:3-5.

brethren, and the goblet would subsequently be handed round so that each in turn might drink to his neighbor. A similar usage, it may be added, still survives at the Corporation banquets of the City of London. The purpose, in both cases, is to re-affirm fraternal solidarity.

Practices of this kind are not confined, however, to single families or brotherhoods. The kinship which is renewed at New Year extends also to all members of the community; for it is, after all, the entire communal unit, and not only the individual households within it, that is entering upon a new lease on life. The *exchange of food* is therefore an equally prominent feature of the celebrations.

In Northumberland (England), for example, a special point is made of visiting neighbors on New Year's Day in order to eat rich cake and drink wine with them. This is called "fadging," though the origin of the term is quite obscure. Similarly, at Coventry, small triangular tartlets filled with mincemeat are sent around as presents. These are known as "god-cakes"—a term which is to be explained from the fact that, in ancient times, persons united by ties of kindred or friendship were known as "gossips," i.e., god-sibs.*

The most familiar example of this exchange of food is, however, the eating of so-called wassail cakes and the quaffing of wassail bowls—the name "wassail" being derived from the old Gaelic *was hael,* "good health," the traditional form of toast. The full-dress ceremony is described in an account dating from the early part of the

* The usage survives in the word *godparent,* and Shakespeare, in his *Midsummer Night's Dream,* alludes to the drinking of "the Gossip's Bowl."

nineteenth century. At that time, we are told, it was customary in Scotland and in the northern counties of England to perform a genteel dance around the table, at the stroke of midnight on New Year's Eve, while the following ditty was chanted:

Weel may we a' be;
Ill may we never see.
Here's to the king
And the guid companie!

The older members of the household would then proceed out of doors, carrying a hot wassail bowl and a lavish supply of wassail cakes for distribution among their neighbors. In this way, communal and social ties were re-cemented for the coming year.

So firmly, indeed, does popular tradition insist on the necessity of eating and drinking together at New Year that, even to this day, the occasion is turned to profitable account by children and poorer folk, who make the rounds of the more wealthy houses, bearing gaily decorated wassail bowls and soliciting pecuniary recognition or due meed of refreshment in such doggerel verses as the following:

Wassail! Wassail! all over the town,
Our toast it is white, our ale it is brown:
Our bowl it is made of a maplin tree;
We be good fellows all: I drink to thee.

Here's to our horse, and to his right ear;
God send our maister a happy New Year;
A happy New Year as e'er he did see—
With my wassailing bowl I drink to thee.

Here's to our mare, and to her right eye;
God send our mistress a good Christmas pie,
A good Christmas pie as e'er I did see—
With my wassailing bowl I drink to thee.

Here's to Fillpail* and to her long tail;
God send our maister as never may fail
Of a cup of good beer: I pray you draw near
And our jolly wassail it's then you shall hear.

Be here any maids? I suppose there be some;
Sure they won't let young men stand on the cold
    stone;
Sing hey, O maids, come trole† back the pin,
And the fairest maid let us all in.

Come, butler, bring us a bowl of the best;
I hope your soul in heaven will rest;
But if you do bring us a bowl of the small,
Then down fall butler, bowl, and all!

or this:

Our jolly wassail bowl,
   A wassail of good ale;
Well fare the butler's soul
   That setteth this to sail—
     Our jolly wassail bowl.

Good dame, here at your door
   Our wassail we begin;

* The name of a cow.
† roll.

We are all maidens poor,
  We pray now let us in
    With our wassail.

Our wassail do we fill
  With apples and with spice;
Then grant us your good will
  To taste here once or twice
    Of our good wassail.

But here they let us stand
  All freezing in the cold.
Good master, give command
  To enter and be bold
    With our wassail.

Much joy into this hall
  With us is entered in.
Our master first of all
  We hope will now begin
    Of our wassail!

Less hale and hearty in tone and more calculated to wring the withers of even the most stony-hearted curmudgeon is the song chanted by poor children:

Here come we a-wassailing,
  Among the leaves so green;
Here we come a-wandering,
  So fair to be seen.

Chorus:

Love and joy come to you,
And to your wassail too,

And God send you a happy New Year, a New Year,
And God send you a happy New Year!
Our wassail-cup is made of rosemary-tree,
So is your beer of the best barley.

We are not daily beggars,
   That beg from door to door,
But we are neighbors' children,
   Whom you have seen before.

Call up the butler of this house,
   Put on his golden ring,
Let him bring us up a glass of beer,
   And the better we shall sing.

We have got a little purse,
   Made of stretching leather skin;
We want a little of your money
   To line it well within.

Bring us out a table
   And spread it with a cloth;
Bring us out a moldy cheese,
   And some of your Christmas loaf.

God bless the master of this house,
   Likewise the mistress too,
And all the little children
   That round the table go!

Good master and good mistress,
   While you're sitting by the fire,
Pray think of us poor children,
   Who are wandering in the mire.
                       Chorus.

It should be added that, if the serenaders go un-rewarded, there is a traditional method of taking reprisals: they pile up a heap of stones outside the door and pronounce over it a solemn curse on the niggardly master of the house!

If the ceremony is to be performed correctly, the contents of the wassail bowl or "hot pint," as it is called, have to be prepared in accordance with traditional specifications. The recipe is thus set forth in an old English newspaper:

> Simmer a small quantity of the following spices in a teacupfull of water, viz.:—Cardamums, cloves, nutmeg, mace, ginger, cinnamon, and coriander. When done, put the spice in two, four, or six bottles of port, sherry, or madeira, with one pound and a half of fine loaf sugar (pounded) to four bottles, and set all on the fire in a clean bright saucepan; meanwhile, have yolks of twelve and whites of six eggs whisked up in it. Then, when the spice and sugared wine is a little warm, take out one teacupful; and so on for three or four cups; after which, when it boils, add the whole of the remainder, pouring it in gradually, and stirring it briskly all the time, so as to froth it. The moment a fine froth is obtained, toss in twelve fine roasted apples, and send it up hot.
>
> Spices for each bottle of wine: 10 grains of mace, 46 grains of cloves, 37 grains of cardamums, 28 grains of cinnamon, 12 grains of nutmeg, 48 grains of ginger, 49 grains of coriander seeds.

Analogous to the wassail is the Quaaltagh, observed

on the Isle of Man. Parties of young men go the rounds
from house to house chanting doggerel verses and demanding entertainment. A typical Quaaltagh song, translated from the Manx, runs as follows:

May they of potatoes and herrings have plenty,
With butter and cheese and each other dainty.

New Year is also characterized, all over the world, by
special foods chosen for symbolic reasons. A favorite dish
is honey. The Romans, for example, used to eat honey
"out of snowhite jars" on January 1; and to this day no
Jewish New Year celebration is complete without the
traditional apples dipped in honey. In popular belief,
this is taken to symbolize the hope that the coming
year may be filled with sweetness. Originally, however, it
possessed a far deeper significance. For in all ancient
religion and folklore, honey was regarded as the primary
means of regeneration; and it is still used in popular
medicine as a cure for almost every type of ailment. The
gods fed on honey and were thereby rendered immortal
and free from disease. The rivers of Paradise were rivers
of honey; and it was, in fact, in pointed allusion to this
that the Promised Land of the Israelites was so often
described as "a land flowing with milk and honey." In
the mythology of the ancient Canaanites, when Baal,
the god of rainfall, returned annually to the earth, after
his long exile during the dry summer months, the event
was said to be heralded by the fact that the wadis
suddenly became filled with honey; and the Greeks
believed that when Dionysus first revealed himself on the
slopes of Mount Parnassus, the rivers ran with honey.

The consumption of honey at New Year was therefore, in the first place, a method of achieving new life and of procuring immunity from sickness. In precisely the same way, honey was served to the initiates in many of the ancient "mystery" religions; and among the Babylonians and Assyrians, libations of honey were poured at the dedication of new sanctuaries. In all of these cases, what it symbolized was entry upon a new lease on life, and such was also its fundamental significance as a New Year dish.

Symbolism appears also in the widespread custom of baking New Year bread and cakes in special shapes. In Swabia, for instance, they are fashioned into rings, representing the cycle of the year; and in the Eifel district of Germany, *Wecken,* or "French rolls," are eaten for the same reason. Among Jews, the loaf used in the ceremony of Sanctification (*Kiddush*) on New Year is usually baked in circular form, to signify the rounded and complete year which is hoped for.

Sometimes, too, the symbolism of New Year fare is of an even more bizarre character. Thus, it is (or was) a common Jewish practice to eat the head of a calf or ram as the *pièce de résistance* of the New Year meal, in order that one may (or might) always come *to the top* during the ensuing twelve months! Similarly, because fishes are everywhere symbolic of teeming abundance, it is customary in Mecklenburg (Germany) and in several other parts of the world to eat fish at New Year as a charm for the increase of riches. Even the color of certain foods is taken as symbolic; white cabbage, for instance, betokens acquisition of silver, and carrots, of gold.

An extreme example of such fantastic symbolism is afforded by the Jewish custom of selecting particular foods because their Hebrew names suggest auspicious omens. Thus—to translate the point into English—leeks are eaten so that enmity and hostility may *leak* away; beets, so that enemies may be *beaten* down; caraway seeds, so that sin may be *carried away;* and cress, so that virtue may in*crease!*

The symbolic character of New Year fare is brought out not only in the selection of dishes but also in the way they are consumed. In Switzerland, a favorite New Year delicacy is sweet whipped cream; but when it is eaten a small portion is spattered on the carpet, and the stain is allowed to remain throughout the year as a token of fatness and increase. Similarly, in Bukovina (Rumania) and in the villages around Tarnopol (Galicia), it is customary to spill some of the New Year gruel on the floor. If it sticks, this is a sign that the bees will likewise stick together in the hive and that there will be plenty of honey. Furthermore, it is regarded as essential, in many parts of the world, that something of the meal eaten on New Year's Eve be left over for the morning, so that the blessings which accrue from it may be repeated. To this end, it is a common practice in Münster (Germany) to wrap up a small portion of the bread and salt and leave it on the table overnight.

In Bohemia, it is customary to substitute beer and wine for the milder drink usually taken for refreshment at "elevenses" in the morning. This is called "drinking to the new blood." Elsewhere, the practice prevails of drinking in the morning for health, in the afternoon for strength, and in the evening for beauty. Similarly, it is standard procedure in some parts of the world to place a lump of sugar under the pillow upon retiring on New Year's Eve. After midnight, the traditional "shooting in" of the year begins; and if anyone hears the first shot before he has nibbled a bit of the sugar, this is a bad omen.

Finally, a word should be said about the taboos imposed upon particular foods at New Year. Many Chinese abstain from the usual bowl of rice on this occasion, in order to distinguish the day from all others. In Hessen, it is believed that if one eats apples on New Year's Day, one will be plagued with sores and itches during the year; and elsewhere in Germany, no dumplings are eaten, lest one's body become disfigured by lumps! The most curious of such is, however, the Jewish proscription of nuts. The reason for this is that every Hebrew letter possesses a numerical as well as an alphabetical value, and those which make up the Hebrew word for "nut" add up (not without a little juggling) to the same total as those which form the word for "sin." To eat nuts is therefore tantamount to absorbing sin.

∽13∽

Gifts and Greetings

As the Vulgar are always very careful to End the *old Year* well, so they are also careful of Beginning well the *new one:* As they End the Former with a hearty Compotation, so they begin the latter with the sending of Presents, which are termed New-Year's Gifts, to their Friends and Acquaintances: the Original of both of which customs is superstitious and sinful; and was observed that the succeeding Year might be prosperous and successful.

HENRY BOURNE, *Antiquitates Vulgares (1725)*

ONE OF THE OLDEST OF NEW YEAR CUSTOMS IS THAT OF exchanging gifts. The custom goes back to the Romans, who used to send one another tokens of luck and good fortune on January 1. These were called *strenae* or "omens" —a word which survives in the French *jour d'étrennes*, the popular name for New Year's Day. They were not regarded as formal presents, but merely as favors or trinkets, and usually took the form of a gilded date or a small coin. Poorer folk who had enjoyed the bounty of wealthy patrons during the course of the year were expected to send them such *strenae* as a mark of attention, and it was likewise the duty of every loyal citizen to make such a gift to the Emperor. Indeed, it is related that in the reign of Augustus people of all ranks used to bring them to the Capitol, even when the Emperor was not there to receive them, or else toss them into the Lacus Curtius with a prayer for his welfare.

What began, however, as an innocent expression of goodwill was turned by the later emperors into a veritable "racket" and soon degenerated into barefaced extortion. Suetonius, the candid biographer of these worthies, tells us, for example, that in order to raise funds for his daughter's education and dowry, the notorious Caligula (12-41 A.D.) actually made a practice of standing in the vestibule of his palace on New Year's Day and himself collecting the contributions which a motley crowd showered upon him by the handful and lapful; his successors increased the exaction to such an outrageous extent that in 395 the relatively honest brothers, Arcadius and Honorius, emperors respectively of the East and West, were obliged to issue a decree formally limiting the amount, and in 458 Pope Leo the Great abolished the practice altogether.

Centuries later, however, the English sovereigns fell back upon the same device as a ready means of swelling their coffers. The chronicler Matthew of Paris relates that in 1249 Henry III, "exceeding the legitimate bounds of kingship," formally extorted a New Year's tribute from the wealthier citizens of London; and a parchment roll of 1584 records that the Archbishop of Canterbury was obliged in that year to present forty pounds, and the lords temporal sums varying from ten to thirty pounds, as a New Year's gift to Queen Elizabeth. The peeresses, adds the account, were required to contribute gowns, bracelets and bejeweled caskets, while the royal physician offered a box of imported candy, the apothecary a packet of lozenges, and the master-cook confections of marzipan and macaroon. Of similar tenor, too, is an entry in the famous Diary of Samuel Pepys: "I had been early this morning," says that redoubtable gossip, "at Whitehall, at the Jewell Office, to choose a piece of gilt plate for my lord [the Earl of Sandwich] in return of his offering to the king (which, it seems, is usual at this time of year, and an earl gives twenty pieces of gold in a purse to the king)."

On at least one occasion, however, the fleeced subject was able to take a subtle revenge on his royal master; for it is recorded of Bishop Latimer that, being obliged to pay the New Year tribute to the profligate Henry the Eighth, he substituted for a cash offering the gift of a Bible heavily marked at The Epistle to the Hebrews 13:4. That verse reads: *Let marriage be had in honour among all, and let the bed be undefiled; for fornicators and adulterers God will judge!*

Nor was it only upon royalty that such tokens were bestowed on New Year's Day. A curious pamphlet published in London in 1647 and advocating the establishment of a university in that city, bears a dedication to the Lord Mayor, aldermen and members of the Common

Council stating that it is presented to them "instead of heathenish and superstitious New Year's gifts."

Similarly, in country districts, peasants and tenantry used to present New Year tribute to the lords of the manor. An interesting account of this custom, as observed in some of the towns of Yorkshire during the early part of the nineteenth century, is contained in Thomas Blount's *Ancient Tenures of Land* (1815), and may here be quoted in full:

> On New Year's Day, annually, the lord of the manor held his court, where, to preserve the right of estray,* each town's shepherd brought a large apple-pie and a twopenny sweet cake, except the shepherd of Herwick, who paid a sum of sixteen pence and a wooden spoon. In the pie brought by the shepherd of Rainton, an inner one was made filled with prunes. The pies were measured by the bailiff and, if of the required size, were cut into an aliquot number of parts and distributed among the steward, the bailiff, the tenant of the coney-warren and the town's shepherds; if a pie were too small, the bailiff might return it and fine the town. The cakes were divided in the same manner. The bailiff gave to each shepherd a slice of cheese and a penny roll, and provided a furmety and mustard, which was put into an earthen pot placed in a hole in the ground. The bailiff provided wooden spoons for the steward, the tenant of the coney-warren and himself; the shepherds provided their own wooden spoons. The steward took a large spoonful of the mixture, and the others followed in

* *right of estray:* grazing rights.

due order; then a glass of ale, paid for by the sixteen pence brought by the shepherd of Herwick, was served to each. Finally, all adjourned to the bailiff's house, and the further business of the court was transacted.

More often, however, the tribute consisted of a fatted capon—a custom satirized by the poet Abraham Cowley (1618-1667) in the following quaint lines:

Ye used in former days to fall
Prostrate to your landlord in his hall,
When with low legs, and in an humble guise,
Ye offer'd up a capon-sacrifice
Unto his worship, at a New Year's tide.

In some parts of Germany, children wait upon their teachers on New Year's Day and present them with small tokens of esteem. This, however, is probably a survival of the ancient Roman custom of paying the salaries of instructors on January 1.

Sometimes, the bearers of New Year tributes were rewarded with a trivial gift. A manuscript book of 1624 containing the household accounts of a certain Sir John Francklyn records the following disbursements:

Item to the musicians on New Year's Day
   in the morning . . . . 1s. 6d.
Item to the woman which brought the apple
   stuck with nuts . . . . 1s. 0d.
Item to the boy who brought two capons . 1s. 0d.
Item paid for the [wassail] cup . . . . 1s. 6d.

Again, it was customary, until the beginning of the

nineteenth century, to place a crown piece under the plate of each of the two English Court chaplains on New Year's Day; and at the present time, a special list of those whom the king has delighted to honor with baronies, knighthoods and other distinctions is published regularly on January 1.

New Year gifts were also exchanged among persons of less exalted social rank. The ancient Persians used to send one another gifts of eggs, the egg being a symbol of regeneration. The early Britons are said to have distributed twigs of mistletoe, this plant being considered a panacea for all sicknesses and a potent averter of demons and witches.

Elsewhere, apples were (and still are) especially favored as New Year's gifts, the reason being, in all probability, that the apple is a symbol of fertility. In Gloucestershire (England), for example, the typical New Year gift is an apple set on three wooden legs and having a sprig of box hung with hazel nuts, the whole resembling a miniature Christmas tree. This is called a *callening*, but the origin of the term is uncertain. Also, in Herefordshire, Worcestershire and sundry other counties, the traditional New Year present is a small pyramid made of leaves, apples, nuts and other fruits, all gilded. (This, of course, is a direct descendant of the Roman gilded date.) At Hastings, Sussex, apples, nuts, oranges and money are thrown out of the windows on New Year's Day, to be scrambled for by the fisher boys and men; and in Nottinghamshire, groups of children used to go the rounds presenting to their friends an apple or orange stuck with cloves or rosemary.

In Friesen, Germany, peasants bring their girl friends

A Callening

a coffee ring or twisted loaf on New Year's Eve. This is kept until Twelfth Night, when the ardent swain returns with a bottle of wine, and the couple partakes of the fare together.

The sending of New Year's gifts was regarded by the Church as a relic of heathen superstition, and no fewer than four Catholic Councils roundly denounced the practice. The ground of the objection, however, was that they were usually accompanied by riotous and unseemly revels, considered unsuitable to the solemnity of the day. When these latter fell into the discard, the attitude of the Church softened perceptibly, and it may now best be summed up in the quaint words of the antiquary Bourne:

> For tho' the ancient Fathers did vehemently invey against the Observation of the Calends of January; yet it was not because of those Presents and Tokens of mutual Affection and Love that passed; but because the Day itself was dedicated to Idols, and because of some prophane Rites and Ceremonies they observed in solemizing it. If, then, I send a New Year's Gift to my Friend, it shall be a Token of my Friendship; if to my Benefactor, a Token of my Gratitude; if to the Poor (which at this Time must not be forgot), it shall be to make their Hearts sing for Joy, and give Praise and Adoration to *the Giver of all good Gifts.*

An attenuated form of the New Year gift is the New Year card. In Western countries, this is a more or less recent innovation, due largely to commercial enterprise. In China, however, New Year cards have existed for more than a thousand years, though in a form very different from our own. The original Chinese New Year cards were really ceremonial visiting cards. Instead of bearing a greeting to the recipient, they bore the name, address and birth date of visitors who came to call on New Year's Day, and they were taken home again after the visit.

Finally, there is the New Year greeting—the least substantial, though often the most effusive, of all tokens of goodwill. Prescribed forms of greeting are attested already in the Middle Ages, and probably go back to magical formulas calculated just as much to forefend demons as to express cordiality. In Korea, it is customary to employ two forms of greeting: one on New Year's Eve, the other on New Year's Day; and the ceremonial recita-

Here be-gins a gweed New Year, Be sooth-in', be sooth-in',

Joy an' peace an' a' be here, An' a-

wa' by Lun-non toon — ie.

New Year greeting sung by fishwives in Collieston, Scotland

tion of the latter is regarded as very important and as something far more than a courtesy.

In some parts of the world, New Year's Day serves also as an occasion for exchanging greetings "in reverse." In country districts of Germany, for example, suitors who have been jilted by their girl friends hang straw fillets instead of floral wreaths outside the latter's door.

～14～

The Old Gray Mare

A PECULIAR AND PUZZLING NEW YEAR CUSTOM, PREVALENT in several parts of the world, is that of dressing up as animals or parading in animal skins.

The most familiar form of this custom is that known as *hodening* or *riding the hobby-horse*. In certain villages of Westphalia (Germany), for instance, it is customary for a grotesque figure, with blackened face and wearing a headgear adorned with hen's feathers, to break in upon the local taverns shortly before midnight on New Year's Eve and "give the signal." At once, pandemonium breaks loose. The assembled villagers mount their hobby-horses (each draped with a white sheet) and race up and down the streets until they reach the house of some more wealthy peasant. If he refuses to entertain them, they proceed to "raise cain" in his backyard. The ceremony is known as "Riding the Gray Mare."

A similar usage prevails in Wales, where the hobby-horse is likewise known as Mari Lwyd or "Gray Mare." It is also current, during the crucial season between Christmas Eve and Twelfth Night, in the English counties of Kent, Essex and Lancashire, and is thus described by a contributor to *The Church Times* of 1891:

> When I was a boy, some forty-five years since, it was always the custom, on Christmas Eve, with the male farm-servants from every farm in our parish of Hoath, and neighboring parishes of Herne and Chislet [in Kent], to go round in the evening from house to house with the hoodining horse, which consisted of the imitation of a horse's head, made of wood, life-size, fixed on a stick about the length of a broom-handle. The lower jaw of the head was made to open with hinges; a hole was made through the roof of the mouth, then another through the forehead, coming out by the throat; through this was passed a cord attached to the lower jaw, which, when pulled by the cord at the throat, caused it to close and open; on the lower jaw large-headed hobnails were driven in to form the teeth. The strongest of the lads was selected for the horse; he stooped, and made as long a back as he could, supporting himself by the stick carrying the head; then he was covered with a horsecloth, and one of his companions mounted his back. The horse had a bridle and reins. Then com-

menced the kicking, rearing, jumping, etc., and the banging together of the teeth.

The accompanying paraders go from house to house, ringing the bell or knocking and demanding a gratuity.

Sometimes, to be sure, the horse takes a somewhat more grotesque form. A lighted candle is placed in the hollow head, in order to create an eerie effect; and in Stuckenborg, Germany, the real skull of a horse is used.

The hobby-horse, however, is not the only form of animal "guising" at New Year. In Tokyo, children dressed as lions are led through the streets by an adult and encouraged to "awaken the New Year" by incessant "roaring"; and in Kyoto, a man dressed as a white fox with a wagging tail is paraded through the city on New Year's Day. Similarly, the Rumanians of Macedonia believe that the Callicanzari, monsters who are half men and half beast, roam around between Christmas and Epiphany; and it is quite common for boys and girls to dress up in their likeness. So common, indeed, is this custom of animal "guising" that, as early as the seventh century, Archbishop Theodore prescribed, in his *Penitential,* special penances for "any who, on the Kalends of January, clothe themselves with the skins of cattle and carry heads of animals." The practice, said that stern ecclesiastic, was nothing short of "devilish (*daemoniacum*)."

Devilish it may well be, but what does it mean? On this the doctors disagree. Most authorities content themselves with the cautious statement that the custom of hodening would seem to be derived from some primitive horse-dance or horse-ritual. Obviously, however, this carries us precisely nowhere until that dance or ritual has been more clearly identified and described. Nor, indeed, would it appear likely that the particular phenomenon of the hobby-horse should be so sharply distinguished from the other forms of animal guising on exactly the same date. It may be suggested, therefore, that the custom is of a piece with the ancient Greek practice of donning fawn skins and other animal pelts at the festivals of Dionysus and that it is also reflected in the mythological tradition which identifies the followers of that god with centaurs—that is, half men and half horse—and with such similar hybrid creatures as satyrs and silenoi. The original purpose of the disguise may well have been to simulate the monstrous and demonic beings who were thought to be especially rampant at the time of the New Year and of the major seasonal festivals.

It should be observed, however, that, in actual practice, the real origin of the custom has been so far forgotten that it is sometimes even assimilated to what is really a quite different seasonal usage—namely, the pantomime of the death and resurrection of fertility. This comes out very clearly, for example, in the hobby-horse ceremony observed annually, on May 1, at Padstow, in Somerset (England). The procession with "the 'Oss" is there accompanied by the chanting of a lilting melody known as the Night Song:

> Unite, unite, let us all unite,
> For Summer is a-comin' today.
> And whither we are going let us all unite
>   On the merry morning of May.

Andante

U -nite u - nite, let us all u - nite For

Sum - mer is a - com- in' to day And

whi - ther we are go - ing let us all u-

nite on the me r-ry morn- ing of May.

"At intervals," we are told, "the tune changes to the slower and no less beautiful 'Day Song,' the words of which, unfortunately, have lost any sense they may once have had:

> Oh, where is King George, oh where is he, oh?
> He's down in his long boat, all on the salt sea, oh.
> Up flies the kite, and down falls the lark.
> There was an old woman, she had an old ewe,
> But she died in her own park, oh.

Adagio rubato

Oh where is King George - oh where's he oh? He's

down in his long boat All on the salt sea

oh Up flies the kite and down falls the

lark There was an old wo - man she had an old

ewe But she died in her own park oh.

While this is being sung, the 'Oss sinks down as though expiring and the teazer (see page 62) pats him caressingly with his club. Then, with a sudden bound, he is on his feet again and dancing madly as the "Night Song" bursts forth once more:

Up Merry Spring, and up the merry ring,
For Summer is a-comin' in today.
How happy are those little birds that merrily do sing
  On the merry morning of May.

Here, quite clearly, the horse has come to be identified with the familiar figure of the dying and reviving spirit of fertility. The Old Gray Mare, she ain't what she used to be.

ᴐ15ᴏ

The Oldest New Year

THE EARLIEST DESCRIPTION OF A NEW YEAR FESTIVAL KNOWN
to us comes from ancient Mesopotamia. It is inscribed in
wedge-shaped characters on a series of clay tablets which,
though themselves of considerably later date, record a
program of ceremonies performed at Babylon since the
remote days of the second millennium B.C.

The festival was celebrated in the month of the vernal
equinox, and lasted from the new moon until the eleventh
day. Our account of the proceedings begins with the
second day.

Two hours before dawn, the high priest arose, washed
in the sacred waters of the Tigris and Euphrates, and
proceeded to the holiest chapel in the main temple, called
Esagila, "the Lofty House." There he drew back a
curtain which screened the image of Marduk, god of the

city, and then addressed him in a long hymn wherein
he was hailed as the re-emergent sun:

> Lord, unto whose high splendor none aspire,
> Lord, O Lord of earth, benignant sire,
> Lord, by whom all the gods are well bested,
> Lord, at whose assault strong men fall dead;
> Lord of kings, O light of all mankind,
> By whom the fate of all things is defined.
> O Lord, to dwell in Babylon dost deem;
> Thy crown Borsippa is, across the stream.
> Thy body, Lord, are yonder farflung skies;
> O Lord, thou seest all things with thine eyes.
> Through thy strong arm all power is brought low,
> And with thy glance thy favor dost bestow.
>
> Thy sunlight, Lord, o'er men dost thou disperse,
> That they thy deeds exalted may rehearse.
>
> .   .   .   .
>
> This House of Light Abundant is thy shrine,
> Lord of the earth, and with those arms of thine
> Dost thou uphold the falling.
> Grant thy grace
> To Babylon thy city; turn thy face
> To Esagila, thy most holy place!

The doors of the temple were then flung open, and the
regular priests, choristers and sacristans entered in. A
threefold prayer was addressed to Marduk, bidding him
ward off all enemies and adversaries.

On the *third* day, the service began in the same
manner. In the forenoon, however, a carpenter, gold-

smith, mason and weaver came into the temple and there
fashioned and clothed two small wooden effigies, one of
cedar wood, the other of tamarisk wood. Each was
adorned with gold and precious stones and stoled in a
red gown. The one held in his left hand a serpent carved
out of cedar wood, the other a scorpion. Both held their
right hands upraised.

On the *fourth* day, the high priest rose three and
one half hours before dawn, washed in the waters of the
sacred rivers, and proceeded to the chapel wherein stood
the images of Marduk and his consort Zarpanitu. Drawing back the curtain, he again addressed the god as the
re-emergent sun and as the establisher of order and
prosperity:

> Lord of all mortals, king of the divine,
> Who dost the pattern of the world define,
> Awful, exalted, lofty and most high,
> Who wieldest kingship, holdest sovereignty,
>
> Marduk, light resplendent, who dost deign
> Here in this House of Light to set thy fane.
> Who spannest heaven, settest earth below,
> Gatherest the seas, and makest green things grow.
> . . . .
> Who dost confer the mace of sovereignty
> Upon the king who stands in awe of thee!

Then, turning to the goddess, he hailed her as the star
Venus, shining resplendent in the twilight:

> She stands, a silver glory in the night,

Brightest of stars, the goddess rob'd in light.
No goddess to her splendor can come nigh,
A shining radiance in the starlit sky!
Lady, we are thy pensioners; oh, plead
Our cause with Marduk, yea, and intercede
To give us life! So shall we praise thy name,
Extol thy works, bear witness to thy fame!

The high priest then proceeded to the great courtyard,
turned his face towards the north, and invoked a threefold blessing on the temple. In this prayer, he addressed
himself especially to the constellation of the Ram—a rem-
iniscence of the fact that New Year's Day had originally
been celebrated at the heliacal rising of Aries. The gates
of the sanctuary were then flung open, and the clergy
admitted.

In the evening, the high priest took up a position in
front of the image of Marduk and recited the so-called
Epic of Creation, from beginning to end. This poem
related how, in the gray dawn of the world, Marduk had
defeated the rebel monster Tiamat and had therefore
been awarded sovereignty over the gods, installed in
Esagila (especially built for him) and from that lofty
eminence proceeded to ordain the world order. The
purpose of the recitation was not only to explain how he
had come to occupy that shrine but also to emphasize
the fact that each New Year was, in fact, a repetition of
those primordial events. (In the opinion of many scholars,
the recital was accompanied by an appropriate panto-
mimic performance.)

On the *fifth* day, the high priest rose even earlier—
four hours before dawn—washed in the sacred waters

and again addressed Marduk and Zarpanitu in the afore-
said manner. This time, however, their astral character
was more pointedly stressed, the god being roundly
identified with Sirius, brightest of stars.

Jupiter, who portents doth ordain,
He is my Lord. My Lord, be thou assuag'd!
Mercury, who sendeth down the rain,
He is my Lord. My Lord, be thou assuag'd!
Saturn, the star of justice and of right,
He is my Lord. My Lord, be thou assuag'd!
Mars, the raging fire of the night,
He is my Lord. My Lord, be thou assuag'd!

Sirius, brightest star, who all transcends—
Where earth begins, and where the ocean ends,
He is my Lord. My Lord, be thou assuag'd!

In a similar vein, Zarpanitu was identified both with
Venus and with the Heavenly Bow, a constellation which
the Babylonians recognized by combining certain stars
of our own Canis Major with others of the neighboring
group of Puppis:

Queen of mercy, be assuag'd!
Lady, be no more enrag'd!

Venus, of all stars most bright,
"My Lady" is her name.

Bow which layeth low all might,
"My Lady" is her name.

The doors of the temple were then flung open. When

the morning offering had been duly presented, a rite of purgation took place. Under the supervision of the high priest, a sacred sorcerer sprinkled the lintels of the building with holy water drawn from the Euphrates and Tigris, smeared them with oil of cedar, burned incense, and beat a tattoo on a bronze kettle-drum in order to scare off demons. Next, a slaughterer came forward and beheaded a ram. The sorcerer then took the severed rump of the animal and rubbed it against the walls, thereby transferring to it any noxiousness or contagion which might be infesting the sacred edifice. (The ceremony was called *kuppuru*—a word which reappears in the familiar Jewish Yom Kippur.) This done, both head and rump were tossed into a stream; and the two officiants, regarded as contaminated, were banished from the precincts of the city until the termination of the festival.

Shortly afterwards, a special chapel was prepared for the reception of Nabu, god of Borsippa, across the river, who was expected to arrive imminently in order to take part, as a visiting dignitary, in that Great Parade which was to constitute the high point of the entire celebration.

A peculiar ceremony now took place. The king was conducted to Esagila by a retinue of priests. On arrival, he was left standing in front of the image of Marduk.

Presently, the high priest came upon the scene, divested him of his crown, scepter and other insignia and deposited them before the statue. Then he slapped the king's face, pulled his ears and forced him to his knees. In this position, the king recited a kind of "negative confession," protesting his innocence of all offenses against the honor of the gods or the welfare of the city. The high priest then declared, on behalf of Marduk, that the confession was accepted, and the royal regalia were restored.

In the evening, a white bull was offered to Marduk while high priest and king together sang a hymn beginning:

O Bull divine, effulgent light,
Whose splendor streams across the night!

(This ceremony was evidently a survival of the days, before 2000 B.C., when the regnant zodiacal sign of the month was the Bull rather than the Ram, as later became the case.)

The program of the remaining days is, unfortunately, lost to us. While, however, we cannot be sure of their sequence, some of the characteristic acts are known.

The outstanding feature of the sixth day was the arrival from Borsippa of the statue of Nabu, accompanied by other gods. This was conveyed by bark from across the river and was installed in the specially prepared chapel. When it arrived, the two wooden effigies which had been fashioned three days earlier were ceremonially burned in its presence; but the significance of the act remains obscure.

The Babylonian New Year festival was characterized also by the performance of a mummers' play representing the passion and resurrection of the god of fertility. This figure, most familiar to us as Tammuz, was identified with Marduk, deity of the city. He was portrayed as divested of his clothing and imprisoned in the great mountain of the netherworld, where two watchmen kept guard over him. During his absence, the city fell into uproar and disorder, and fighting took place within it—a clear projection into mythology of the saturnalian revels and the ritual combat which elsewhere mark the end of the year.[*] His consort Beltis ("the Goddess") went in search of him, like Demeter for Persephone, and he was eventually retrieved.

Another feature of the ceremonies was the celebration of a so-called "sacred marriage" between Marduk and his consort Zarpanitu. The purpose of this ceremony was to increase fertility; and it is probable that the parts of bride and groom were played respectively by a sacred prostitute and by the king.

It was at New Year, too, that the destinies of the world were determined. The gods were believed to convene for the purpose in a special chamber of Esagila called the Chamber of Fates. This was located in that part of the temple which had been reserved for the god Nabu, the reason being that Nabu was the registrar of the heavenly court, who recorded on clay tablets the good and evil deeds of men. Indeed, it was primarily to discharge this function that he came to Babylon for the occasion.

Lastly, the festival was marked by a sumptuous parade of the divine images from the Chamber of Fates in Esagila to a special edifice known as the "New Year house" on the outskirts of the city. The journey was made on chariots, through a special "Processional Street" to a point on the River Euphrates where the images were loaded upon barges. They remained in the "New Year house" from the eighth until the eleventh day of the celebrations, but the precise purpose of their sojourn is

[*] See page 32ff.

obscure. On the eleventh day, the return trip was made, and on the morrow the deities went back to their native cities.

There is reason to suppose that the formal religious ceremonies were accompanied by festivities of a more popular character. These took the form of a kind of carnival, distinguished by the wearing of masks and the performance of mummeries, and characterized by a saturnalian inversion of the normal order of things, masters waiting upon slaves and mistresses upon handmaids. It is probable also—though the evidence is inconclusive—that, as in many other parts of the world, a condemned criminal reigned during this season as an *interrex*, or deputy king—a prototype of the latter-day Lord of Misrule and King of the Carnival.*

Variations of the Babylonian New Year ceremonies are attested also from the ancient Mesopotamian cities of Erech and Asshur, the native gods taking the place, of course, of the Babylonian Marduk. At Asshur, in fact, the remains of the "New Year house" have actually been excavated. On its bronze door is engraved a picture of the god Assur's fight against the dragon of chaos and other monsters, suggesting that this battle was acted out in pantomime as part of the ceremonies.

* See page 17ff.

❧16❧

Rosh Hashanah[*]

FEW NEW YEAR FESTIVALS ARE MORE IMPRESSIVE OR MORE significant than that observed by Jews at the end of September or the beginning of October.

The Jewish month is determined by the moon, and the year is reckoned in two ways. For most civil and legal purposes—such as the dating of marriage contracts and other records—it begins in spring, at the new moon of Nisan, preceding the barley harvest and the vernal solstice. For religious purposes, however, it is measured from the new moon of Tishri, preceding the ingathering of fruits and the autumnal equinox.

[*] The following account is based on traditional practice, as preserved among orthodox and conservative Jews. Reform Jews have discarded many of the ancient usages and have introduced several modifications and innovations both in observance and in doctrine.

The new year of Nisan is not kept as a formal holiday. That of Tishri, however, inaugurates the most solemn period in the entire Jewish calendar—namely, the ten great Days of Awe which culminate in the Day of Atonement (Yom Kippur). Not only is this New Year the anniversary of the world's creation but it is also—and more importantly—an annual Day of Judgment, when the deeds of all flesh are passed in review before God and the fate of all living is decided for the ensuing twelve months.

Originally, the year began with the Feast of Ingathering at full moon. The first of Tishri was simply the beginning of a preliminary festal period—a kind of Hebrew Yuletide. That period opened in a spirit of mortification and austerity, expressed by various abstinences and taboos and by a partial suspension of the normal order of life. Then it passed into a phase of purification and absolution, the tenth day being signalized as the Day of Purgations or Atonement (*Yom ha-kippurim*) and distinguished by ceremonies designed to cleanse the community of sin and contagion and to remove evil influences. Finally it issued in a general jubilation, coincident with the gathering of the fruit harvest.

In the Bible, the opening day of this sacred season is known only as the Day of Memorial.* What this meant is, however, altogether obscure. According to some scholars, it was the day on which the creation of the world and the major events of the past were solemnly recalled and perhaps even acted out in pantomime. According to others, it was a commemoration of the dead, such as usually takes place at the beginning of the agricultural year.†

* Exodus 12:14; Leviticus 23:24.
† See Chapter 9.

The occasion would appear to have been characterized by three principal themes, namely: the forefending of evil spirits; the installation of God as King of the world; and the determination of destinies for the ensuing twelve-month.

In order to avert demons and "princes of darkness," it was customary to sound the *shofar* or ram's horn. This was, of course, of the same order as the widespread custom of tooting horns, ringing bells, clanging gongs, and generally creating pandemonium on New Year's Eve and on similar seasonal festivals. Indeed, it is significant that the trumpets were in fact sounded not only on the Day of Memorial but also *at every new moon,** for in the belief of most peoples throughout the world, the dark o' the moon is the time when malevolent beings are especially rampant.

The installation of the Divine King at this season is nowhere expressly mentioned in the Old Testament. We know, however, that this was a cardinal element of the New Year celebrations among neighboring peoples. The Babylonians, as we have seen, believed that the god Marduk then defeated the rival forces of chaos and thereby acquired sovereignty over gods and men;† and a document of the fourteenth century B.C., recently discovered in North Syria, would seem to indicate that among the Canaanites, Baal, god of the rains, was thought to fight his way to kingship at the beginning of autumn by defeating Death and the Dragon of the Sea. That the Israelites likewise possessed this myth—if only as an element of folklore—is shown by several passages of the

* Numbers 10:10.
† See Chapter 15.

Bible which refer to Jehovah's primordial combat with Leviathan or some similar monster of the deep, and it is significant that in most of these passages his triumph is connected closely with the establishment of the world order. In the Ninety-third Psalm, for example, the impressive declaration "Jehovah is become king" is followed immediately by the statement that he is "mightier than the mighty waters," and that by subduing the raging streams he has stabilized the world, set his own throne on a solid foundation, and issued "sure testimonies," i.e., promulgated the cosmic order. Similar also is Psalm 74:12-17:

> God is my King from of old,
> Working salvation in the midst of the earth.
> 'Twas Thou didst break Sir Sea in pieces by Thy
> strength,
> Didst shatter the heads of the dragons in the waters.
> 'Twas Thou didst crush the heads of Leviathan,
> Didst give him to be food to the sharks of the sea.*
> 'Twas Thou didst cleave fountain and brook;
> 'Twas Thou didst dry up perennial streams.
> Thine is the day, Thine also is the night;
> Sun and luminary—'Twas Thou didst establish them.
> 'Twas Thou didst set all the borders of the earth;
> 'Twas Thou didst make summer and winter.

Moreover, that this victory and enthronement were connected with the autumnal festival is strongly suggested

---

* The English Bible renders, "to the people inhabiting the wilderness;" but it is generally recognized that the Hebrew text is here corrupt, and our translation represents the standard correction of it.

by the fact that both the First and the Second Temple (i.e., the "palaces" of Jehovah) were actually consecrated at the Feast of Ingathering;* while in Zechariah 14:16, pilgrims to that festival are described as coming to Jerusalem to pay homage to "the King, the Lord of Hosts."

The belief that human destinies were determined at New Year was, of course, simply a corollary of the common idea that the beginning of a new agricultural cycle was, in fact, a renewal of creation.

The Jewish festival of Rosh Hashanah represents a remarkable transformation and sublimation of these primitive beliefs and usages.

Whatever its original significance may have been, the Day of Memorial is now regarded as the day on which God remembers the good and evil deeds of men and metes out rewards and punishments for them. It is also the day on which He calls to mind the virtues of the ancient patriarchs, mercifully allowing them to offset the sins and transgressions of their descendants. Finally, it is the day on which both God and Israel remind themselves of their mutual obligations under the Covenant concluded at Mount Sinai.

Similarly, the blowing of the shofar is now taken as a signal to the "army of the Lord" to march ever forward and, if need be, do battle in His name. It is a reminder also of things past and of things to come—of the trumpet blasts which "grew louder and louder" when the Law was given at Mount Sinai (Exodus 19:16) and of the ultimate redemption of Israel on the day when "the Lord God will blow the ram's horn, and go with the

* I Kings 8:2; Nehemiah 8:13-18.

whirlwinds of the south" (Zechariah 9:14). Finally, it is a presage of the Last Trump which will be sounded at the resurrection of the dead.

The sovereignty of God likewise remains a cardinal theme of the festival. The mythological setting has, to be sure, long since disappeared; there is no longer any reference to the fight with Leviathan nor any mimetic representation of the enthronement. Throughout the statutory prayers, however, references to the "holy God" are systematically changed to read "holy King," and frequent allusion is made to the advent of the day when "the Lord shall be King over all the earth." As one of the better-known hymns expresses it:

All the world shall come to serve Thee
And bless Thy glorious Name,
And Thy righteousness triumphant
The islands shall acclaim.
And the peoples shall go seeking
Who knew Thee not before,
And the ends of earth shall praise Thee,
And tell Thy greatness o'er.

They shall build for Thee their altars,
Their idols overthrown,
And their graven gods shall shame them,
As they turn to Thee alone.
They shall worship Thee at sunrise,
And feel Thy Kingdom's might,
And impart their understanding
To those astray in night.

They shall testify Thy greatness,
And of Thy power speak,
And extol Thee, shrined, uplifted
Beyond man's highest peak.
And with reverential homage,
Of love and wonder born,
With the ruler's crown of beauty
Thy head they shall adorn.

With the coming of Thy kingdom
The world shall break in song,
And the islands laugh exultant
That they to God belong.
And all their congregations
So loud Thy praise shall sing,
That the uttermost peoples, hearing,
Shall hail Thee crownèd King.*

Moreover, the sounding of the shofar is interpreted also as a royal fanfaron and is introduced by the words, "With trumpets and sound of the ram's horn blow a blast before the King, Jehovah" (Psalms 98:6).

The central motif of Rosh Hashanah is, however, that of the Day of Judgment. On this day, says tradition, all who enter the world pass before the Heavenly Judge like troops in a review or like sheep beneath the shepherd's crook. God opens His great book and records the fate of each according to his deserts: "Who is to live and who to die, who to rest and who to rove, who to grow rich and who to grow poor." A variant account asserts, how-

* The poem was written by Eleazar Kalir in the ninth century. The translation is by Israel Zangwill.

ever, that *three* books are opened: one for the wholly righteous, who are straightway inscribed for life; one for the wholly wicked, who are straightway inscribed for death; and a third for the intermediate class, whose fate is not finally sealed until the Day of Atonement. During the interval, they are given the opportunity of repenting their evil ways, for "prayer, penitence and charity may avert the evil decree." In reference to this belief, the customary greeting on Rosh Hashanah is "May you be inscribed for a good year."

All of these ideas are caught up in the formal service of the synagogue. The most familiar element of that

Blowing the Shofar

service is the ceremonial blowing of the *shofar*, which is repeated four times. On the first three occasions, it is associated respectively with the kingship of God, the remembrance of sins and transgressions, and the recollection of past deliverances, and is introduced in each case by the recitation of appropriate verses from the Bible. The order of notes is determined by rigid tradition, and consists in combinations of three basic sounds, namely, *tekiah*, a short bass note ending abruptly; *teru'ah*, a long blast; and *shebarim*, a series of quavers or trills. The musical scheme is as follows:

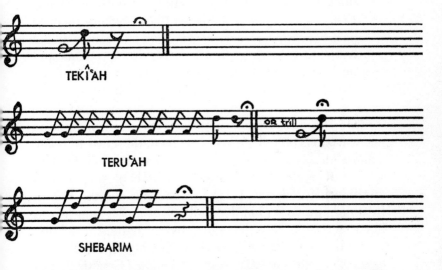

TEKÎAH

TERU'AH

SHEBARIM

The theme of divine judgment is stressed especially in the so-called Additional Morning Service (*Musaf*), which now takes the place of the extra sacrifices offered on this day in the Tabernacle and Temple. The most famous element of this service is the solemn chanting of the hymn entitled *Unetanneh Tokef* ("Now let us recite the majesty of this day"), in which God is represented as sitting in heavenly assize, while all mankind pass before him in judgment:

> The great trumpet is blown, and a still small voice is heard. The angels quiver in fright; fear and trembling seize them. And they cry one to another: Behold, the Day of Judgment is here, when the hosts on high shall be visited with judgment, for even they are not guiltless in God's eyes. And all that enter the world shall pass before Him as troops in review. Even as a shepherd tends his flock, making them to pass beneath his crook, so shall God make every living being to pass beneath His gaze, as He counts and numbers and tells them, and sets His brand upon all creation, and seals the doom of each.

Into the traditional structure of the festival Judaism has woven certain elements of its own, designed to relate it more closely to the particular history of Israel. On this day, it is averred, the patriarch Abraham prepared to sacrifice his only son Isaac in obedience to the test of fidelity imposed on him by God (Genesis 22); and it was likewise on this day that the prophet Samuel was born.

Both events are reflected in the liturgy of the occasion. The story of Abraham's devotion (Genesis 21-22) is read as the primary lesson from the Law; and on the first day of the festival, the story of the birth of Samuel (I Samuel 1:1-2:10) serves as the reading from the Prophets. Moreover, it is held by tradition that the sounding of the ram's horn is intended, among other things, to recall the miraculous substitution of a ram at the moment when Abraham was on the point of slaying his son. Indeed, it is customary in the Sephardic (Spanish and Portuguese) rite to preface the first blasts of the shofar with the chanting of a long poem on this theme written, in the twelfth century, by Samuel ibn Abbas, rabbi of Fez, Morocco. The poem is set to a rousing tune, with the refrain:

> Remember the binder,
> Remember the bounden,
> Remember the altar!

Nor is it only in the formal services of the synagogue that the spirit of the occasion is expressed. On the afternoon of the festival, observant Jews make a point of going to the nearest river or lake and throwing into it crumbs emptied out of their pockets, the while they intone in Hebrew the concluding verses of the Book of Micah:

> God will again have compassion upon us,
>   tread our iniquities under foot;
> Yea, Thou wilt cast all their sins into the depths of
>   the sea,
> showing faithfulness unto Jacob, mercy unto Abra-
>   ham,
> Even as Thou swarest to our fathers from days of
>   old.*

This, of course, is simply a variation on the familiar

* The ceremony is known as *Tashlich*—the Hebrew word for "Thou wilt cast."

practice of consigning evil and impurity to the waters at the beginning of the year.* Characteristically, however, Judaism has placed its own stamp upon the time-honored usage; for in Judaism, all religious acts are related immediately to the perpetuation of the Covenant and to the abiding memory and virtue of the patriarchs who walked with God. The promise of the new and changing year thus becomes the fulfillment of the old and eternal pledge.

* See page 41ff.

∾17∾

Janus

New year looks both backwards and forwards. On the one hand, it is the birthday of the world; on the other, it is the model of that new and better order which is destined to follow the present age. Both ideas are caught up in the popular lore associated with the day.

On New Year's Day the same things are repeated as took place on the first of all New Years, at the very dawn of creation. Once again, the god goes forth to battle against the dragon of chaos, to rein the demon of the rising waters, to establish the order of the world and to determine the destinies of mankind. For the process of creation is continuous, and the universe is reborn from year to year: *magnus ab integro saeclorum nascitur*

Janus

ordo. * The whole purpose of the sacred pantomime which so frequently characterizes New Year celebrations is, indeed, to effect this new beginning; it is not merely an artistic portrayal of what happened in the past, but a positive and actual repetition of it.

By the same token, the various elements of the New Year program set the pattern for what may be expected at the last of all New Years—the great "day of the Lord" which will usher in the dawn of a new era and the beginning of life abounding.

Once again—to follow the descriptions given in the Bible—God will go forth to do battle with the Evil One: "In that day the Lord with His sore and great and strong sword shall punish Leviathan the swift serpent and Leviathan the crooked serpent; and He shall slay the

* "The great sequence of the ages is born anew." Vergil, *Eclogues,* iv:5.

Dragon that is in the sea" (Isaiah 27:1). Once again He will engage in combat against the rebellious and the refractory: "The Lord shall go forth and fight against the nations, as when He fought in the day of battle" (Zechariah 14:3). And once again, by subduing those fell adversaries, He will fight His way to kingship: "And the Lord shall be king over all the earth; in that day shall the Lord be one, and His name one" (Zechariah 14:9). On that day, the trumpet will again resound, and the dead will again awaken and return to the living:"We shall not all sleep, but we shall be changed, in a moment, in the twinkling of an eye, at the last trump; for the trumpet shall sound, and the dead shall be raised incorruptible" (I Corinthians 15:51-52). Then, too, God will sit in judgment—even as He does at each New Year —and the destinies of the good and the evil will be determined. Then, too, He will celebrate His reunion with the faithful by joining them in the traditional New Year meal. But this time, He will be host, not guest: "And ... the Lord of Hosts shall make unto all peoples a feast of fat things, a feast of wines on the lees, of fat things full of marrow, of wines on the lees well refined. And He will destroy ... the face of the covering that is cast over all peoples, and the veil that is spread over all nations. He shall swallow up Death for ever; and the Lord God will wipe away tears from off all faces" (Isaiah 25:6-8). Finally, on that day, the long night of vigil will be ended, and salvation will come with the rising sun: "Unto you that fear My name shall the sun of righteousness arise with healing in his wings" (Malachi 4:2).

The First Day and the Last Day are New Years. As it was in the beginning, is now, and ever shall be, world without end, Amen.

Now the new year reviving old desires
The thoughtful soul to solitude retires.

Rubáiyat of Omar Khayyám

Bibliography

MOST GOOD TRAVEL BOOKS INCLUDE DESCRIPTIONS OF NATIVE
New Year customs, and it is mainly through extensive reading
in this branch of literature that an adequate picture of their
nature and significance can be acquired. There are, however,
a number of short-cuts.

First and foremost is Sir James Frazer's *The Golden Bough*,
which may be consulted, for convenience, in the inexpensive
one-volume edition. Even though Frazer's conclusions are no
longer accepted by the majority of specialists, his immense
collection of material remains unrivaled. Then, for those who
read German, there is Paul Sartori's invaluable *Sitte und
Brauch* (3 vols., Leipzig: 1910-14), which, though it concen-
trates primarily on German usages, often adduces parallels
from other parts of the world and thus constitutes a veritable
mine of information.

The English and Scottish customs are described in John
Brand's famous *Observations on the Popular Antiquities of
Great Britain* (ed. H. Ellis, 2 vols., London: 1902) and in
the Folk-Lore Society's volumes, *British Calendar Customs:
England*, vol. ii (ed. A. R. Wright and T. E. Lones, London:
1938) and *British Calendar Customs: Scotland*, vol. ii (ed.
M. M. Banks, London: 1938).

The Mohammedan New Year ('Ashura) is admirably de-
scribed in Chapter xxiv of E. W. Lane's classic *Manners and
Customs of the Modern Egyptians* (available in Everyman's
Library). Other accounts may be found in E. Westermarck's
Pagan Survivals in Mohammedan Civilisation (London: 1933),

pp. 145 ff., and in G. E. von Grunebaum's *Mohammedan Festivals* (in this series).

The best source on the Jewish New Year is H. Schauss' *The Jewish Festivals* (Cincinnati: 1928), pp. 112-24, 143-49; and S. Agnon's beautiful anthology, *Days of Awe* (New York: 1949), brings together most of what is to be found on the subject in Jewish literature and traditional lore. From the critical and historical point of view, the best treatment of the Jewish New Year, and especially of its earlier Biblical prototype, is N. H. Snaith's *The Jewish New Year Festival* (London: 1947). The tractate of the Mishnah dealing with New Year may be read in H. Danby's translation (Oxford: 1933), while the liturgy is most readily accessible in the standard Adler and Davis edition, which includes verse renderings by Nina Salaman and Israel Zangwill.

The ritual of the Babylonian New Year (Akîtu) festival has been most recently translated by A. Sachs in the volume, *Ancient Near Eastern Texts relating to the Old Testament* (Princeton: 1950), pp. 331-34. The original texts are published, with translations and notes, in F. Thureau-Dangin's French volume, *Rituels accadiens* (Paris: 1921). They are discussed in detail in S. A. Pallis' *The Babylonian Akîtu Festival* (Copenhagen: 1926). A convenient summary, by C. J. Gadd, is included in *Myth and Ritual* (ed. S. H. Hooke, London: 1933).

The Persian New Year (Nauruz) is described by C. K. Naruman in his article, "Armaghan Nawruz Khosrawi: description of the Sassanian New Year's Day," in the *Bulletin of the Iranian League*, 1931. Another good account is in J. E. Polak's *Persien, das Land und seine Bewohner* (Leipzig: 1865), vol. i, pp. 367-89. It is summarized in English in R. Patai's *Man and Temple* (London: 1947), pp. 80-83.

On the Chinese New Year, see: W. Eberhard, *Chinese Festivals* (in this series) and J. Bredon and I. Mitrophanow,

The Moon Year: A Record of Chinese Customs and Festivals (Shanghai: 1927).

The Japanese New Year is described in H. C. Gunsaulus, *The Japanese New Year's Festival* (Chicago: 1923). See also: W. H. Erskine, *Japanese Festival and Calendar Lore* (Tokyo: 1934).

Hindu New Year cermonies are discussed in B. A. Gupta, *Hindu Holidays and Ceremonials* (Calcutta: 1919).

On primitive methods of gauging time, the standard work is M. Nilson's *Primitive Time-Reckoning* (Lund: 1920). A more popular treatment is contained in S. H. Hooke's booklet, *New Year's Day* (London: 1922).

The general background of the "seasonal pattern" is discussed, with abundant examples, in the present writer's *Thespis: Ritual, Myth and Drama in the Ancient Near East* (New York: 1950).

Valuable also are the articles on "Festivals and Fasts" in Hastings' *Encyclopaedia of Religion and Ethics*; for particular customs the reader may consult the new *Standard Dictionary of Folklore, Mythology and Legend* (2 vols., New York: 1949-50) and such older works as Chambers' *The Book of Days* (London-Edinburgh: 1866) and W. S. Walsh's *Curiosities of Popular Customs* (various editions).

Index

Abbas, Samuel ibn, poem by, 123
Abbot, The, 18
Abruzzi, and *Pietro Rico,* 24
Algonquins, unit of time of, 1
Altair, reckoning of season by, 4
Amur River, medicine men of, and bells, 49
Ancient Tenures of Land, quoted, 88-89
Anthesteria, festival of, 52
Antiquitates Vulgares, 85
Arabs, and bells, 49
Arcadia, and Pan, 39
Arcadius, and New Year gifts, 86
Armenians, and Feast of the Transfiguration, 42
'Ashura festival, 22, 42
Asshur, New Year ceremonies in, 111
Assyrians, and honey, 81
astronomical phenomena, measuring of seasons by, 3
Attis, death and resurrection of, 14, 55
Austria, banishment of death in, 20
Aztecs, and "unfit for work" days, 14

Babe, as symbol of New Year, 67-70
Babylonians: and honey, 81; and new clothes, 58; and New Year festival, 15, 103-111; observance of "lent" by, 13-14; reckoning of year by, 4; and revisiting of the dead, 52; scapegoats and, 29
Bakitara of Uganda Protectorate, and temporary king, 15

Bali, revisiting of dead in, 53
Barea, Hebrides, scapegoat in, 28
Bastar, and temporary king, 15
Bavaria, and New Year omens, 64
Belgium, beating of fruit trees in, 38
Bibliomancy, 62
Blount, Thomas, quoted, 88
Bogos of Abyssinia, and ringing of bells, 48
Bohemia: banishment of death in, 20; expelling evil in, 29-30; and New Year drinks, 82
Borneo, seasons in, 2
Boswell, and Cyprian passion, 9
Brandenburg, and New Year's Day, 58
Bourne, Henry, quoted, 85, 92
Burma: New Year festival in, 12; rites of cleansing in, 42
Busk festival, 58-59

calendar, establishing of, 1-6
Caligula, and New Year gifts, 86
callening, 90
Cambodia: abdication of king in, 15; New Year in, 12
Cambridge University, and Lord of Misrule, 17
Canaanite poem, 25-26
Carinthia, combat in, 31
Cherokees, and New Year festival, 12
China: and New Year cards, 92; and New Year food, 83; noise-making in, 47
Christ Child, 69
Christmas (Yuletide), 13, 18, 23, 29, 32, 33, 38, 61, 63, 69, 96, 97